THE PHILOSOPHY OF ART.

ART

IN THE

NETHERLANDS

BY

H. TAINE

TRANSLATED BY

J. DURAND

NEW YORK:

LEYPOLDT & HOLT.

1871.

Entered according to Act of Congress, in the year 1870, by

LEYPOLDT & HOLT,

in the Office of the Librarian of Congress at Washington.

STEREOTYPED BY
DENNIS BRO'S & THORNE,
AUBURN, N. Y.

PRESS OF
THE NEW YORK PRINTING COMPANY,
81, 83, and 85 Centre Street,
NEW YORK.

TO

GUSTAVE FLAUBERT.

SYNOPSIS OF CONTENTS.

PART I.—PERMANENT CAUSES.

PART II.—HISTORIC EPOCHS.

PART I.

PERMANENT CAUSES.

THE PHILOSOPHY OF ART IN THE NETHERLANDS.

DURING the last three years I have explained to you the history of painting in Italy; this year I propose to set before you the history of painting in the Netherlands.

Two groups of mankind have been, and still are, the principal factors of modern civilization; on the one hand, the Latin or Latinized people—the Italians, French, Spanish and Portuguese, and on the other, the Germanic people—the Belgians, Dutch, Germans, Danes, Swedes, Norwegians, English, Scotch and Americans. In the Latin group the Italians are undeniably the best artists; in the Germanic group they are indisputably the Flemings and the Dutch. In studying, accordingly, the history of art along with these two races, we are studying the history of modern art with its greatest and most opposite representatives.

A product so vast and varied, an art enduring nearly four hundred years, an art enumerating so many masterpieces and imprinting on all its works an original and common character, is a national product; it is consequently intimately associated with the national life, and is rooted in the national character itself. It is a flowering long and deeply matured through a development of vitality conformably to the acquired structure and primitive organization of the plant. According to our method we shall first study the innate and preliminary history which explains the outward and final history. I shall first show you the seed, that is to say the race, with its fundamental and indelible qualities, those that persist through all circumstances and in all climates; and next the plant, that is to say the people itself, with its original qualities expanded or contracted, in any case grafted on and transformed by its surroundings and its history; and finally the flower, that is to say the art, and especially painting, in which this development culminates.

I.

The men who inhabit the Netherlands belong, for the most part, to that race which invaded the Roman empire in the fifth century, and which then, for the first time, claimed its place in broad sunshine alongside of Latin nations. In certain countries, in Gaul, Spain and Italy, it simply brought chiefs and a supplement to the primitive population. In other countries, as in England and the Netherlands, it drove out, destroyed and replaced the ancient inhabitants, its blood, pure, or almost pure, still flowing in the veins of the men now occupying the same soil. Throughout the middle ages the Netherlands were called Low Germany. The Belgic and Dutch languages are dialects of the German, and, except in the Walloon district, where a corrupt French is spoken, they form the popular idiom of the whole country.

Let us consider the common characteristics of the Germanic race, and the differences by which it is opposed to the Latin race. Physically, we have a whiter and softer skin, generally speaking, blue eyes, often of a porcelain or pale hue, paler as you approach the north, and sometimes glassy in Holland; hair of a flaxy blonde, and, with children, almost white; the ancient Romans early wondered at it, and stated that infants in Germany had the hair of old men. The complexion is of a charming rose, infinitely delicate among young girls, and lively and tinged with vermilion among young men, and sometimes even among the aged; ordinarily, however, among the laboring classes and in advanced life I have found it wan, turnip-hued, and in Holland cheese-colored, and mouldy cheese at that. The body is generally large, but thick-set or burly, heavy and inelegant. In a similar manner the features are apt to be irregular, especially in Holland, where they are flabby, with projecting cheekbones and strongly-marked jaws. They lack, in short, sculptural nobleness and delicacy. You will rarely find the features regular like the numerous pretty faces of Toulouse and Bordeaux, or like the spirited and handsome heads which abound in the vicinity of Rome and Florence. You will much oftener find exaggerated features, incoherent combinations of form and tones, curious fleshy protuberances, so many natural caricatures. Taking them for works of art, living forms testify to a clumsy and fantastic hand through their more incorrect and weaker drawing.

Observe now this body in action, and you will find its animal faculties and necessities of a grosser kind than among the Latins; matter and mass seem to predominate over motion and spirit; it is voracious and even carnivorous. Compare the appetite of an Englishman, or even a Hollander, with that of a Frenchman or an Italian; those among you who have visited the country can call to mind the public dinner tables and the quantities of food, especially meat, tranquilly swallowed several times a day by a citizen of London, Rotterdam or Antwerp. In English novels people are always lunching—the most sentimental heroine, at the end of the third volume, having consumed an infinite number of buttered muffins, cups of tea, bits of chicken, and sandwiches. The climate contributes to this; in the fogs of the north, people could not sustain themselves, like a peasant of the Latin race, on a bowl of soup or a piece of bread flavored with garlic, or on a plate of macaroni. For the same reason the German is fond of potent beverages. Tacitus had already remarked it, and Ludovico Guiccardini, an eye-witness in the sixteenth century, whom I shall repeatedly quote, says, in speaking of the Belgians and Hollanders : " Almost all are addicted to drunkenness, which vice, with them, is a passion. They fill themselves with liquor every evening, and even at day-break." At the present time, in America and in Europe, in most of the German countries, intemperance is the national bane; half of the suicides and mental maladies flow from it. Even among the reflective and those in good circumstances the fondness for liquor is very great : in Germany and in England it is not regarded as disreputable for a well-educated man to rise from the table partially intoxicated ; now and then he becomes completely drunk. With us, on the contrary, it is a reproach, in Italy a disgrace, and in Spain, during the last century, the name of drunkard was an insult which a duel could not wholly wipe out, provoking, as it often did, the dagger. There is nothing of

this sort in German countries; hence the great number and frequency of breweries and the innumerable
shops for the retailing of ardent spirits and different
kinds of beer, all bearing witness to the public taste.
Enter, in Amsterdam, one of these little shops, garnished with polished casks, where glass after glass is
swallowed of white, yellow, green and brown brandy,
strengthened with pepper and pimento. Place yourself at nine o'clock in the evening in a Brussels
brewery, near a dark wooden table around which
the hawkers of crabs, salted rolls and hard-boiled
eggs circulate; observe the people quietly seated
there, each one intent on himself, sometimes in
couples, but generally silent, smoking, eating, and
drinking bumpers of beer which they now and then
warm up with a glass of spirits; you can understand
sympathetically the strong sensation of heat and
animal plenitude which they feel in their speechless
solitude, in proportion as superabundant solid and
liquid nourishment renews in them the living substance, and as the whole body partakes in the grati-
fication of the satisfied stomach.

One point more of their exterior remains to be

shown which especially strikes people of southern
climes, and that is the sluggishness and torpidity of
their impressions and movements. An umbrella-
dealer of Amsterdam, a Toulousian, almost threw
himself into my arms on hearing me speak French,
and for a quarter of an hour I had to listen to the
story of his griefs. To a temperament as lively as
his, the people of this country were intolerable—
"stiff, frigid, with no sensibility or sentiment, dull
and insipid, perfect turnips, sir, perfect turnips!"
And, truly, his cackling and expansiveness formed a
contrast. It seems, on addressing them, as if they
did not quite comprehend you, or that they required
time to set their expressional machinery agoing;
the keeper of a gallery, a household servant, stands
gaping at you a minute before answering. In coffee-
houses and in public conveyances the phlegm and
passivity of their features are remarkable; they do
not feel as we do the necessity of moving about
and talking — they remain stationary for hours,
absorbed with their own ideas or with their pipes.
At evening parties in Amsterdam, ladies, bedecked
like shrines, and motionless on their chairs, seem to

be statues. In Belgium, in Germany and in England, the faces of the peasantry seem to us inanimate, devitalized or benumbed. •A friend, returning from Berlin, remarked to me, " those people all have dead eyes." Even the young girls look simple and drowsy. Many a time have I paused before a shop-window to contemplate some rosy, placid and candid face, a mediæval madonna making up the fashions. It is the very reverse of this in our land and in Italy, where the grisette's eyes seem to be gossiping with the chairs for lack of something better, and where a thought, the moment it is born, translates itself into gesture. In Germanic lands the channels of sensation and expression seem to be obstructed; delicacy, impulsiveness, and readiness of action appear impossible; a southerner has to exclaim at their awkwardness and lack of adroitness, and this was the deliberate opinion of our French in the wars of the Revolution and the Empire. In this respect the toilette and deportment afford us the best indications, especially if we take the middle and lower classes of society. Compare the grisettes of Rome, Bologna, Paris and Toulouse with the huge mechanical dolls to be seen at Hampton Court on Sundays, starched and stiff in their blue scarfs, staring silks and gilded belts, and other details of a pompous extravagance. I remember at this moment two fêtes—one at Amsterdam to which the rich peasant women of Friesland flocked, their heads decked with a fluted cap and a hat like a cabriolet rearing itself convulsively, whilst on the temples and brow were two gold plates, a gold pediment and gold corkscrews surrounding a wan and distorted countenance ; the other at Fribourg, in Brisgau, where, planted on their solid feet, the village women stood vaguely staring at us and exhibiting themselves in their national costume—so many black, red, purple and green skirts, with stiff folds like those of gothic statues, a swollen corsage front and rear, massive sleeves puffed out like legs of mutton, forms girded close under the armpits, dull, yellow hair twisted into a knot and drawn towards the top of the head, chignons in a net of gold and silver embroidery, and above this a man's hat, like an orange-colored pipe, the heteroclite crown of a body seemingly hewn out with a cleaver, and vaguely suggesting a painted sign-post. In brief, the human animal of this race is more passive and more gross than the other. One is tempted to regard him as inferior on comparing him with the Italian or southern Frenchman, so temperate, so quick intellectually, who is naturally apt in expression, in chatting and in pantomine, possessing taste and attaining to elegance, and who, without effort, like the Provençals of the twelfth, and the Florentines of the fourteenth century, become cultivated, civilized and accomplished at the first effort.

We must not confine ourselves to this first glance which presents only one phase of things; there is another associated with it, as light accompanies dark. This finesse, and this precocity, natural to the Latin families, leads to many bad results. It is the source of their craving for agreeable sensations; they are exacting in their comforts; they demand many and varied pleasures, whether coarse or refined, an entertaining conversation, the amenities of politeness, the satisfactions of vanity, the sensualities of love, the delights of novelty and of accident, the harmonious symmetries of form and of phrase; they readily develope into rhetoricians, dilettanti, epicureans, voluptuaries, libertines, gallants and worldlings. It is indeed through these vices that their civilization becomes corrupt or ends; you encounter them in the decline of ancient Greece and Rome, in Provençe of the twelfth, in Italy of the sixteenth, in Spain of the seventeenth, and in France of the eighteenth centuries. Their more quickly cultivated temperament bears them more speedily on to subtleties. Coveting keen emotions, they cannot be happy with moderate ones: they are like people who, accustomed to eating oranges, throw away carrots and turnips; and yet it is carrots and turnips, and other equally insipid vegetables, which make up our ordinary diet. It is in Italy that a noble lady exclaims, on partaking of a delicious ice-cream, "What a pity there is no sin in it!" In France a noble lord remarks, speaking of a diplomatic roué, "Who wouldn't admire him, he is so wicked!" In other directions their vivacity of impression and promptness of action render them improvisators; they are so quickly and so deeply excited by a crisis as to forget duty and reason, resorting to daggers in Italy and Spain, and to pistols in France; showing by this that they are only moderately capable of biding their time, of self-subordination, and of maintaining order. Success in life depends on knowing how to be patient, how to endure drudgery, how to unmake and remake, how to recommence and continue without allowing the tide of anger or the flight of the imagination to arrest or divert the daily effort. In fine, if we compare their faculties with the world as it runs, it is too mechanical, too rude, and too monotonous for them, and they too lively, too delicate, and too brilliant for it. Always after the lapse of centuries this discord shows itself in their civilization; they demand too much of things, and, through their misconduct, fail even to reach that which things might confer on them.

Suppress, now, these fortunate endowments, and, on the dark side, these mischievous tendencies,—imagine on the slow and substantial body of the German a well-organized brain, a sound mind, and trace the effects. With less lively impressions a man thus fashioned will be more collected and more thought-

ful; less solicitous of agreeable emotions, he can, without weariness, do disagreeable things. His senses
being blunter, he prefers depth to form, and truth
within to show without. As he is less impulsive he
is less subject to impatience and to unreasonable out-
bursts; he has an idea of sequence, and can persist
in enterprises the issue of which is of long achieve-
ment. Finally, with him the understanding is the
better master, because outward temptations are
weaker and inward explosions rarer; reason governs
better where there is less inward rebellion and less
outward attack. Consider, in effect, the Germanic
people of the present day and throughout history.
They are, primarily, the great laborers of the world;
in matters of intellect none equal them; in erudition,
in philosophy, in the most crabbed linguistic studies,
in voluminous editions, dictionaries and other compi-
lations, in researches of the laboratory, in all science,
in short, whatever stern and hard, but necessary and
preparatory work there is to be done, that is their
province; patiently, and with most commendable
self-sacrifice they hew out every stone that enters into
the edifice of modern times. In material matters the

English, Americans and Dutch perform the same service. I should like to show you an English spinner or cloth-dresser at work; he is a perfect automaton, occupied day in and day out without a moment's relaxation, and the tenth hour as well as the first. If he is in a workshop with French workmen, these form a striking contrast; they are unable to adapt themselves to the same mechanical regularity; they are sooner tired and inattentive, and thus produce less at the end of the day; instead of eighteen hundred spools, they only turn out twelve hundred. The farther south you go the less the capacity. A Provençal or Italian must gossip, sing and dance; he is a willing lounger, and lives as he can, and in this way easily contents himself with a threadbare coat. Indolence there seems natural and honorable. A *noble life*, the laziness of the man who, to save his honor, lives on expedients, and sometimes fasts, has been the curse of Spain and Italy for the last two hundred years. On the other hand, in the same epoch, the Fleming, the Hollander, the Englishman and the German have gloried in providing themselves with all useful things; the instinctive repugnance

which leads an ordinary man to shun trouble, the
puerile vanity which leads the cultivated man to distinguish himself from the artizan, disappear alongside
of their good sense and reason.

This same reason and this same good sense estab-
lish and maintain amongst them diverse descriptions
of social engagements, and first, the conjugal bond.
You are aware that among the Latin families this is
not over respected; in Italy, Spain and France
adultery is always the principal subject of the play
and the romance ; at all events, literature in these
lands always incarnates passion in the hero, and is
prodigal of sympathy for him by granting him all
privileges. In England, on the contrary, the novel
is a picture of loyal affection and the laudation of
wedlock; in Germany, gallantry is not honorable,
even among students. In Latin countries it is
excused or accepted, and even sometimes approved
of. The matrimonial yoke, and the monotony of the
household, there seem galling. Sensational allure-
ments penetrate too deeply ; the caprices of the
imagination there are too brusque; the mind creates
for itself visions of transports and of ecstatic

delight, or at least a romance of exciting and varied sensuality, and at the first opportunity the suppressed flood bursts forth, carrying with it every barrier of duty and of law. Consider Spain, Italy and France in the sixteenth century; read the tales of Bandello, the comedies of Lope de Vega, the narratives of Brantôme, and listen for a moment to the comment of Guiccardini, a contemporary, on the social habits of the Netherlands. "They hold adultery in horror . . . Their women are extremely circumspect, and are consequently allowed much freedom. They go out alone to make visits, and even journeys without evil report; they are able to take care of themselves. Moreover they are house-keepers, and love their households." Only very lately, again, a wealthy and noble Hollander named to me several young ladies belonging to his family who had no desire to see the Great Exposition, and who remained at home whilst their husbands and brothers visited Paris. A disposition so calm and so sedentary diffuses much happiness throughout domestic life; in the repose of curiosity and of de-sire the ascendancy of pure ideas is much greater;

the constant presence of the same person not being
wearisome, the memory of plighted faith, the sentiment of duty and of self-respect easily prevails
against temptations which elsewhere triumph because they are elsewhere more powerful. I can say
as much of other descriptions of association, and especially of the free assemblage. This, practically, is
a very difficult thing. To make the machine work
regularly, without obstruction, those who compose
it must have calm nerves and be governed by the
end in view. One is expected to be patient in a
'meeting,' to allow himself to be contradicted and
even vilified, await his turn for speaking, reply
with moderation, and submit twenty times in succession to the same argument enlivened with figures
and documentary facts. It will not answer to fling
aside the newspaper the moment its political interest
flags, nor take up politics for the pleasure of discus-
sion and speech-making, nor excite insurrections
against officials the moment they become distasteful,
which is the fashion in Spain and elsewhere. You
yourselves have some knowledge of a country where
the government has been overthrown because in-

active and because the nation felt ennui. Among Germanic populations, people meet together not to talk but to act; politics is a matter to be wisely managed, they bring to bear on it the spirit of business; speech is simply a means, while the effect, however remote, is the end in view. They subordinate themselves to this end, and are full of deference for the persons who represent it. How unique! Here the governed respect the governing; if the latter prove objectionable they are resisted, but legally and patiently; if institutions prove defective, they are gradually reformed without being disrupted. Germanic countries are the patrimony of free parliamentary rule. You see it established today in Sweden, in Norway, in England, in Belgium, in Holland, in Prussia, and even in Austria; the colonists engaged in clearing Australia and the West of America, plant it in their soil, and, however rude the new-comers may be, it prospers at once, and is maintained without difficulty. We find it at the outset in Belgium and Holland; the old cities of the Netherlands were republics, and so maintained themselves throughout the middle ages

in spite of their feudal suzerains. Free communities
arose, and maintained themselves without effort, at
once, the small as well as the great, and in the great
whole. In the sixteenth century we find in each
city, and even in small towns, companies of arquebusiers and rhetoricians, of which more than two hundred have been enumerated. In Belgium to-day
there still flourish an infinity of similar corporations,
societies of archers, of musicians, of pigeon fanciers,
and for singing birds. In Holland volunteer associations of private individuals minister to every
requirement of public charity. To act in a body, no
one person oppressing another, is a wholly Germanic
talent, and one which gives them such an empire
over matter; through patience and reflection they
conform to the laws of physical and human nature,
and instead of opposing them profit by them.

If, now, from action we turn to speculation, that
is to say to the mode of conceiving and figuring
the world, we shall find the same imprint of this
thoughtful and slightly sensualistic genius. The
Latins show a decided taste for the external and
decorative aspect of things, for a pompous display

feeding the senses and vanity, for logical order, outward symmetry and pleasing arrangement, in short,
for form. The Germanic people, on the contrary,
have rather inclined to the inward order of things,
to truth itself, in fact, to the fundamental. Their
instinct leads them to avoid being seduced by
appearances, to remove mystery, to seize the hidden,
even when repugnant and sorrowful, and not to
eliminate or withhold any detail, even when vulgar
and unsightly. Among the many products of this
instinct there are two which place it in full light
through the strongly marked contrast in each of
form and substance, and these are literature and
religion. The literatures of Latin populations are
classic and nearly or remotely allied to Greek poesy,
Roman eloquence, the Italian renaissance, and the
age of Louis XIV.; they refine and ennoble, they
embellish and prune, they systematize and give proportion. Their latest masterpiece is the drama of
Racine, who is the painter of princely ways, court
proprieties, social paragons, and cultivated natures;
the master of an oratorical style, skilful composition and literary elegance. The Germanic litera-

tures, on the contrary, are romantic; their primitive source is the Edda and the ancient sagas of the north; their greatest masterpiece is the drama of Shakespeare, that is to say the crude and complete representation of actual life, with all its atrocious, ignoble and common-place details, its sublime and brutal instincts, the entire outgrowth of human character displayed before us, now in a familiar style bordering on the trivial, and now poetic even to lyricism, always independent of rule, incoherent, excessive, but of an incomparable force, and filling our souls with the warm and palpitating passion of which it is the outcry. In a similar manner take religion, and view it at the critical moment when the people of Europe had to choose their faith, that is to say in the sixteenth century; those who have studied original documents know what this at that time meant; what secret preferences kept some in the ancient faith and led others to take the new one. All Latin populations, up to the last, remained Catholic; they were not willing to renounce their intellectual habits; they remained faithful to tradition; they continued subject to authority; they were affected through sensuous externalities—the pomp of worship, the imposing system of the Catholic hierarchy, the majestic conception of Catholic unity and Catholic perpetuity; they attached absolute importance to the rites, outward works and visible acts through which piety is manifested. Almost all the Germanic nations, on the contrary, became Protestants. If Belgium, which inclined to the Reformation, escaped, it was owing to force through the successes of Farnese, the destruction and flight of so many Protestant families, and to a special moral crisis which you will find in the history of Rubens. All other Germanic peoples subordinated outward to inward worship. They made salvation to consist of a renewal of the heart and of religious sentiment; they made the formal authority of the Church yield to personal convictions; through this predominance of the fundamental form became accessory, worship, daily life and rites being modified in the same degree. We shall soon see that in the arts the same opposition of instincts produced an analogous contrast of taste and style. Meanwhile let it suffice for us to seize the cardinal points which

2*

distinguish the two races. If the latter, compared with the former, presents a less sculpturesque form, grosser appetites and a more torpid temperament, it furnishes through tranquillity of nerve and coolness of blood a stronger hold on pure reason ; its mind, less diverted from the right road by delight in sensuous attractions, the impetuosities of impulse and the illusions of external beauty, is better able to accommodate itself now to comprehend things and now to direct them.

II.

This race, thus endowed, has received various imprints, according to the various conditions of its abiding-place. Sow a number of seeds of the same vegetable species in different soils, under various temperatures, and let them germinate, grow, bear fruit and reproduce themselves indefinitely, each on its own soil, and each will adapt itself to its soil, producing several varieties of the same species so much the more distinct as the contrast is greater between the diverse climates. Such is the experience of the Germanic race in the Netherlands. Ten centuries of habitation have done their work; the end of the middle ages shows us that, in addition to its innate character, there is an acquired character.

It becomes necessary, therefore, to study the soil and the sky; in default of travel take the next best thing, .a map. Excepting the mountainous district to the south-east, the Netherlands consist of a watery plain, formed out of the deposits of three large rivers —the Rhine, the Meuse and the Scheldt, besides several smaller streams. Add to this numerous inlets, ponds and marshes. The country is an outflow of mighty waters, which, as they reach it, become sluggish and remain stagnant for want of a fall. Dig a hole anywhere and water comes. Examine the landscapes of Van der Neer and you will obtain some idea of the vast sluggish streams which, on approaching the sea, become a league wide, and lie asleep, wallowing in their beds like some huge, flat, slimy fish, turbid and feebly glimmering with scaly reflections. The plain is oftentimes below their level, and is only protected by levées of earth. You feel as if some of them were going to give way; a mist is constantly rising from their surfaces, and at night a dense fog envelopes all things in a bluish humidity. Follow them down to the sea, and here a second and more violent inundation, arising from the daily tides, completes the work of the first. The northern ocean is hostile to man. Look at the "Estacade" of Ruysdael, and imagine the frequent tempests casting up ruddy waves and monstrous foaming billows on the low, flat band of earth already half submerged by the enlargement of the rivers. A belt of islands, some of them

equal to the half of a department, indicates, along
the coast, this choking up of inland currents and the
assaults of the sea—Walcheren, North and South
Beveland, Tholen, Schouwen, Voorn, Beierland, Texel,
Vlieland and others. Sometimes the ocean runs up
and forms inner seas like that of Harlem, or deep
gulfs like the Zuyder Zee. If Belgium is an alluvial
expanse, formed by the rivers, Holland is simply a
deposit of mud surrounded by water. Add to all
this an unpropitious soil and a rigorous climate,
and you are tempted to conclude that the country was not made for man but for storks and
beavers.

When the first Germanic tribes came to encamp
here it was still worse. In the time of Cæsar and
Strabo there was nothing but a swampy forest;
travellers narrate that one could pass from tree to
tree over all Holland without touching the ground.
The uprooted oaks falling into the streams formed
rafts, as nowadays on the Mississippi, and barred
the way to the Roman flotillas. The Waal, the
Meuse and the Scheldt annually overflowed their
banks, the water covering the flat country around to

a great distance. Autumnal tempests every year submerged the island of Batavia, while in Holland the line of the coast changed constantly. Rain fell incessantly, and the fog was as impenetrable as in Russian America; daylight lasted only three or four hours. A solid coating of ice annually covered the Rhine. Civilization, meanwhile, as the soil became cleared, tempered the climate; the rude Holland of that day possessed the climate of Norway. Flanders, four centuries after the invasion, was still called "the interminable and merciless forest." In 1197 the country about Waes, now a garden, remained untilled, the monks on it being besieged by wolves. In the fourteenth century droves of wild horses roamed through the forests of Holland. The sea encroached on the land. Ghent was a seaport in the ninth century, Thorout, St. Omer and Bruges in the twelfth century, Damme in the thirteenth, and Ecloo in the fourteenth. On looking at the Holland of old maps we no longer recognize it.* Still, at the present day its inhabitants are obliged to guard the soil against the

---

* Michiels, "Histoire de la Peinture Flamande," Vol. I., p. 230; and Schayes' ' Les Pays-Bas-avant et pendant la domination Romaine."

rivers and the sea. In Belgium the margin of the
sea is below the level of the water at high tide, the
polders or low spots thus reclaimed displaying vast
argillaceous flats, with a slimy soil tinged with purple
reflections, between dykes, which, even in our days,
sometimes break away. The danger in Holland is
still greater, life there seeming to be very precarious.
For thirteen centuries a great inundation has taken
place, on an average, every seven years, besides
smaller ones; one hundred thousand persons were
drowned in 1230, eighty thousand in 1287, twenty
thousand in 1470, thirty thousand in 1570, and twelve
thousand in 1717. Similar disasters occurred in 1776,
in 1808, and still later in 1825. Dollart Bay, about
seven miles wide by twenty deep, and the Zuyder
Zee, forty-four leagues square, are invasions of the
sea in the thirteenth century. In order to protect
Friesland it was necessary to drive three rows of
piles a distance of twenty-two leagues, each pile cost-
ing seven florins. To protect the coast of Harlem
they had to build a dyke of Norway granite five
miles long by forty feet in height, and which is
buried two hundred feet beneath the waves. Am-

sterdam, which has two hundred and sixty thousand inhabitants, is entirely built on piles, frequently thirty feet long. The foundations of every town and village in Friesland are artificial constructions. It is estimated that seven and a half billions of francs have been expended on protective works between the Scheldt and the Dollart. Life has to be purchased in Holland. And when from Harlem or Amsterdam you see the enormous yellow surf beating against that narrow strip of mud, and enclosing it as far as the eye can reach, it is evident that man, in casting this sop to the monster, obtains safety at a low rate.*

Imagine, now, on this quagmire, the ancient Germanic tribes, so many fishers and hunters roaming about in hide boats and clad in seal-skin tunics, and estimate if you can the effort those barbarians were forced to make in order to create a habitable soil and transform themselves into a civilized people. Men of another stamp would not have succeeded; the *milieu* was too unfavorable. In analogous conditions the inferior races of Canada and Russian

---

* See Alphonse Esquiros' "La Néerlande et la Vie Neérlandaise." 2 vols.

America have remained savage; other well-endowed races, the Celts of Ireland and the Highland Scotch, attained only to a chivalric standard of society and poetic legends. Here there had to be good, sound heads, a capacity to subject sensation to thought, to patiently endure ennui and fatigue, to accept privation and labor in view of a remote end, in short a Germanic race, meaning by this men organized to co-operate together, to toil, to struggle, to begin over and over again and ameliorate unceasingly, to dike streams, to oppose tides, to drain the soil, to turn wind, water, flats, and argillaceous mud to account, to build canals, ships and mills, to make brick, raise cattle, and organize various manufacturing and commercial enterprises. The difficulty being very great the mind was absorbed in overcoming it, and, turned wholly in this direction, was diverted from other things. To subsist, to obtain shelter, food and raiment, to protect themselves against cold and damp, to accumulate stores and lay up wealth left the settlers no time to think of other matters; the mind got to be wholly positive and practical. It is impossible in such a country to indulge in revery, to philosophize German fashion, to stray off amidst chimeras of the fancy and through the world of metaphysical systems.* One is immediately brought back to the earth. The necessity of action is too universal, too urgent, too constant; if people think at all, it is to act. Under this steady pressure the character forms; that which was habit becomes instinct; the form acquired by the parent is found hereditary in the child; laborer, artisan, trader, factor, householder, man of common sense and nothing more, he is by birth and without effort what his ancestors got to be through necessity and constraint.†

This positive spirit, moreover, is found to be tranquillized. Compared with other nations of the same stock and with a genius no less practical, the denizen of the Netherlands appears better balanced and more capable of being content. We do not see in him the violent passions, the militant disposition, the overstrained will, the bull-dog instincts, the sombre and

---

* Alfred Michiels' "Histoire de la Peinture," Vol. I., p. 233. This volume contains a number of general views all deserving of attention.

† Prosper Lucas' "De l'Hérédité," and Darwin's "Origin of Species."

grandiose pride which three permanent conquests and
the secular establishment of political strife have implanted in the English ; nor that restless and exaggerated desire for action which a dry atmosphere,
sudden changes from heat to cold, a surplus elec-
tricity, have implanted in the Americans of the
United States. He lives in a moist and equable
climate, one which relaxes the nerves and developes
the lymphatic temperament, which moderates the
insurrections, explosions and impetuosity of the spirit,
soothing the asperities of passion and diverting the
character to the side of sensuality and good humor.
You have already observed this effect of climate in
our comparisons of the genius and the art of the
Venetians with those of the Florentines. Here,
moreover, events come to the aid of climate, history
laboring in the same direction as physiology. The
natives of these countries have not undergone, like
their neighbors over the channel, two or three invasions, the overrunning of an entire people, Saxons,
Danes and Normans installed on their premises ;
they have not garnered a heritage of hatred which
oppression, resistance, rancor, prolonged struggle,

warfare—at first open and violent, and afterwards subdued and legal—transmit from one generation to another. From the earliest times down we find them engaged, as in the age of Pliny, in making salt, "combined together, according to ancient usage, in bringing under cultivation marshy grounds,"* free in their guilds, asserting their independence, claiming their rights and immemorial privileges, devoted to whaling, trade and manufacturing, calling their towns *ports*, in brief, as Guiccardini describes them in the sixteenth century, " very desirous of gain and watchful of profit, but without anything feverish or irrational in their desire to provide for themselves. They are by nature cool and self-possessed. They delight in wealth and other worldly things prudently and as occasion offers, and are not easily disturbed, which is at once apparent both in their discourse and in their physiognomies. They are not prone to anger or to pride, but live together on good terms, and are especially of a gay and lively humor." According to him they entertain no vast and overweening ambi-

---

* Moke's " Mœurs et Usages des Belges," pp. 111, 113. A capitulary of the ninth century.

tion; many of them retire from business early, amusing themselves with building, and taking life easily
and pleasantly. All circumstances, moral and physical, their geographical and political state, the past
and the present, combine to one end, namely, the
development of one faculty and one tendency at the
expense of the rest, shrewd management and temperate emotions, a practical understanding and limited desires; they comprehend the amelioration of
outward things, and, this accomplished, they crave
no more.

Consider, in effect, their work; its perfection and
lacunœ indicate at once the limits and the power of
their intellect. The profound philosophy which is so
natural in Germany, and the elevated poetry which
flourishes in England, they lack. They fail to over-
look material things and positive interests in order
to yield to pure speculation, to follow the temerities
of logic, to attenuate the delicacy of analysis, and
bury themselves in the depths of abstraction. They
ignore that spiritual turmoil, those eruptions of
suppressed feeling which give to style a tragic
accent, and that vagabond fancy, those exquisite

and sublime reveries which outside of life's vulgarities reveal a new universe. They can boast of no great philosopher; their Spinoza is a Jew, a pupil of Descartes and the rabbis, an isolated recluse of a different genius and a different race. None of their books have become European like those of Burns and Camoens, who, nevertheless, were born out of nations equally small. One only of their authors has been read by every man of his epoch, Erasmus, a refined writer but who wrote in Latin, and who, in education, taste, style and ideas belongs to the erudites and humanists of Italy. The old Dutch poets, as for example, Jacob Cats, are grave, sensible, somewhat tedious moralists, who laud home enjoyments and the life of the family. The Flemish poets of the thirteenth and fourteenth centuries tell their auditors that they do not recount chivalric fables—but veritable histories, their poesy ending in practical maxims and contemporary events. In vain do their belle-lettre academies cultivate and make poetry prominent, there being no talent to produce out of such resources any great or beautiful performance. Chroniclers arise like Châtelain, and pamphleteers like Marnix de Sainte-Aldegonde, but their unctuous narratives are inflated; their overcharged eloquence, coarse and crude, recalls, without equalling it, the rude color and vigorous grossness of their national art. They have scarcely any literature at the present day. Their only novelist, Conscience, seems to us, although a tolerable observer, dull and unrefined. If we visit their country and read their journals, those at least not got up in Paris, we seem to have fallen upon the provinces, and even lower. Polemical discussions are gross, the flowers of rhetoric stale, humor rudely indulged, and wit pointless; a coarse joviality and a coarse anger supply the material; their very caricatures seem to us stupid. If we attempt to ascertain their contributions to the great edifice of modern thought we find that patiently and methodically, like honest and faithful workmen, they have hewn out a few blocks. They can point to a learned school of philologists at Leyden, to jurisprudential authorities like Grotius, to naturalists and physicians like Leeuvenhoeck, Swammerdam and Boerhaave, to physicists like Huyghens, and to cosmographers like Ortelius and

Mercator, in short, to a contingent of specialist
and useful men, but to no creative intellect dis-
closing to the world grand original ideas or enshrin-
ing original conceptions in beautiful forms capable
of universal ascendancy. They have left to neighboring nations the part filled by the contemplative
Mary at the feet of Jesus, choosing for themselves
that of Martha; in the seventeenth century they
provided pulpits for the Protestant erudites exiled
from France, a country for free thought persecuted
throughout Europe, and editors for all books of
science and polemics; at a later period they furnished printers for the whole of our eighteenth
century philosophy, and finally booksellers, brokers
and counterfeiters for the entire literature of modern times. All this is of service to them for they
are versed in languages, and read and are instructed, instruction being an acquisition and something which it is good to lay up like other things.
But there they stop, and neither their ancient nor
their modern works show any need of or faculty for
contemplating the abstract beyond the apparent
world and the imaginary world outside of reality.

On the contrary they have always excelled and they still excel in the arts called useful. "First among transalpine people," says Guiccardini, "they invented woolen fabrics." Up to 1404 they alone were capable of weaving and manufacturing them. England supplied them with the raw material, the English doing no more than raise and shear the sheep. At the end of the sixteenth century, an unique thing in Europe, "almost everybody, even the peasantry, could read and write; a great many even acquired the principles of grammar." We find, accordingly, belle-lettre academies, that is to say associations for oratory and dramatic representations, even in the small towns. This indicates the degree of perfection to which they brought their civilization. "They have," says Guiccardini, "a special and happy talent for the ready invention of all sorts of machines, ingenious and suitable for facilitating, shortening and dispatching everything they do, even in the matter of cooking." They, indeed, with the Italians, are the first in Europe to attain to prosperity, wealth, security, liberty, com fort, and all other benefits which seem to us the paraphernalia of modern times. In the thirteenth century Bruges was equal to Venice; in the sixteenth century Antwerp was the industrial and commercial capital of the North. Guiccardini never wearies in praising it, and he only saw it when it was in full decline, reconquered by the Duke of Parma after the terrible siege of 1585. In the seventeenth century Holland, remaining free, occupies for a century the place which England now holds in the world of to-day. It is in vain for Flanders to fall back into Spanish hands, to be ravaged by the wars of Louis XIV., to be surrendered to Austria, to serve as a battle-ground for the wars of the Revolution ; she never descends to the level of Spain or Italy ; the partial prosperity she maintains throughout the miseries of repeated invasion and under a bungling despotism shows the energy of her inspiring good sense and the fecundity of her assiduous labor.

Of all the countries of Europe at the present day, Belgium is the one which with an equal area supports the most inhabitants; she feeds twice as many as France; the most populous of our departments, that of the North, is a portion which Louis XIV detached from her. Towards Lille and Douai you already see spread out in an indefinable circle, ex· tending up to the horizon, this great kitchen garden, a deep and fertile soil diapered with pale grain sheaves, poppy-fields, and the large-leaved beet, and richly stimulated by a low, warm sky swimming with vapor. Between Brussels and Malines begins the broad prairie, here and there striped with rows of poplars, intersected with water-courses and fences, where cattle browse throughout the year, an inex- haustible storehouse of hay, milk, cheese and meat. In the environs of Ghent and Bruges, the land of Waes, " the classic soil of agriculture," is nourished by fertilizers gathered in all countries, and by barn- yard manure brought from Zealand. Holland, in like manner, is simply a pasturage, a natural tillage, which, instead of exhausting the soil, renews it, pro- viding its cultivators with the amplest crops, and affording to the consumer the most strengthening aliments. In Holland, at Buicksloot, there are mil- lionaire cow-herds, the Netherlands ever seeming to the stranger to be a land of feasting and good cheer. If you turn from agricultural to industrial results, you will everywhere encounter the same art of utilizing and making the best of things. Obstacles with them are transformed into aids. The soil was flat and soaked with water; they took advantage of it to cover it with canals and railroads, no place in Europe presenting so many channels of communication and of transport. They were in want of fuel; they dug down into the bowels of the earth, the coal-pits of Belgium being as rich as those of England. The rivers annoyed them with their inundations and inland pools deprived them of a portion of their territory; they drained the pools, diked the streams, and profited by the rich alluvions and the slow deposits of vegetable mould with which the surplus or stagnant waters overspread their land. Their canals freeze up; they take skates and travel in winter five leagues an hour. The sea threatened them; after forcing it back, they avail themselves of it to traffic with all nations. The winds sweep unimpeded across their flat country and over the turbulent ocean; they make them swell the sails of their vessels and move the wings of their windmills. In

Holland you will observe at every turn of the road one of these enormous structures, a hundred feet high, furnished with machinery and pumps, busy in emptying the overflow of water, sawing ship-timber and manufacturing oil. From the steamer, in front of Amsterdam, you see, stretching off as far as the eye can reach, an infinite spider's web, a light, indistinct and complex fringe of masts and arms of windmills encircling the horizon with their innumerable fibres. The impression you carry away is that of a country transformed from end to end by the hand and the art of man, and sometimes entirely created until it becomes a comfortable and productive territory.

Let us go further; let us take a near view of man, and appreciate the most important object belonging to him—his habitation. There is no stone in this country—nothing but an adhesive clay, suitable for men and horses to mire their feet in. It occurred to the people, however, to bake it, and in this way brick and tile, which are the best of defences against humidity, came into their hands. You see well contrived buildings of an agreeable aspect, with red,

brown and rosy walls covered with a bright stucco
white façades varnished and sometimes decorated
with sculptured flowers, animals, medallions and
small columns. In the older cities the house often
stands with its gable to the street, festooned with
arcades, branchings and leafage, which terminate in
a bird, an apple or a bust; it is not, as in our
cities, a continuation of its neighbor—an abstract
compartment of vast barracks, but an object apart,
endowed with a special and private character, at
once interesting and picturesque. Nothing could
be better kept and cleaner. At Douai the poorest
have their domicile whitewashed once a year, outside and in, it being necessary to engage the white-
washer six months in advance. At Antwerp, in
Ghent and in Bruges, and especially in the small
towns, most of the façades seem to be newly painted
or freshened the day before. Washing and sweep-
ing are going on on all sides. When you reach
Holland there is extra care even to exaggera-
tion. You see domestics at five o'clock in the
morning scrubbing the sidewalks. In the environs of Amsterdam the villages seem to be scenery

from the Opera-Comique, so tidy and so well-
dusted are they. There are stables for cows, the
flooring of which is cabinet work; you can enter
them only in slippers or sabots placed at the
entrance for that purpose; a spot of dirt would be
scandalous, and still more so any odor; the cows'
tails are held up by a small cord to prevent them
from soiling themselves. Vehicles are prohibited
from entering the village; the sidewalks of brick
and blue porcelain are more irreproachable than a
vestibule with us. In autumn children come and
gather up the fallen leaves in the streets to deposit
them in a pit. Everywhere, in the small rooms,
seemingly the state-rooms of a ship, the order and
arrangement are the same as on a ship. In Broeck,
it is said, there is in each house a particular room
which is entered only once a week in order to clean
and rub the furniture, and then carefully closed; in
a country so damp, dirt immediately becomes a
deleterious mould; man, compelled to scrupulous
cleanliness, contracts the habit, experiences its necessity, and at last falls under its tyranny. You would
be pleased, however, to see the humblest shop of

the smallest street in Amsterdam, with its brown casks, its immaculate counter, its scoured benches, everything in its place, the economy of small quarters, the intelligent and handy arrangement of all utensils. Guiccardini already remarks "that their houses and clothes are clean, handsome and well-arranged, that they have much furniture, utensils and domestic objects, kept in better order and with a finer lustre than in any other country." It is necessary to see the comfort of their apartments, especially the houses of the middle classes—carpets, waxed cloths for the floors, warm and heat-saving chimneys of iron and porcelain, triple curtains at the windows, clear, dark and highly polished window-panes, vases of flowers and green plants, innumerable knick-knacks indicative of sedentary habits and which render home life pleasant, mirrors placed so as to reflect the people passing in the street together with its changing aspects;—every detail shows some inconvenience remedied, some want satisfied, some pleasant contrivance, some thoughtful provision, in short, the universal reign of a sagacious activity and the extreme of comfort.

Man, in effect, is that which his work indicates.
Thus endowed and thus situated, he enjoys and knows
how to enjoy. The bountiful soil furnishes him with
abundant nutriment — meat, fish, vegetables, beer
and brandy; he eats and drinks copiously, while in
Belgium the Germanic appetite, as it grows in fas-
tidiousness without decreasing, becomes gastronomic
sensuality. Cooking there is scientific and perfect,
even to the hotel tables; I believe that they are the
best in Europe. There is a certain hotel in Mons to
which visitors from the small neighboring towns
come to dine every Saturday, especially to enjoy a
delicate meal. They lack wine, but they import it
from Germany and France, and boast the possession
of the best vintages: we do not, in their opinion,
treat our wines with the respect they deserve; it is
necessary to be a Belgian to care for and relish them
in a proper manner. There is no important hotel
which is not supplied with a varied and select stock;
its reputation and custom are made by the selection;
in the railroad cars the conversation tends sponta-
neously to the merits of two rival cellars. A prudent
merchant will have twelve thousand bottles in his

3*

sanded cellars, duly classified; it constitutes his library. The burgomaster of a petty Dutch town possesses a cask of genuine Johannisberger, made in the best year, and this cask adds to the consideration of its owner. A man there, who gives a dinner party, knows how to make his wines succeed each other in such a way as not to impair the taste and have as many as possible consumed. As to the pleasures of the ear and the eye, they understand them as well as those of the palate and the stomach. They instinctively love the music which we only appreciate through culture. In the sixteenth century they are first in this art; Guiccardini states that their vocalists and instrumentalists are esteemed in all the courts of Christendom; abroad, their professors found schools, and their compositions are standards of authority. Even nowadays the great musical endowment of being able to sing in parts is encountered even amongst the populace; the coal-miners organize choral societies; I have heard laborers in Brussels and Antwerp, and the ship caulkers and sailors of Amsterdam sing in chorus, and in true time, while at work and in the street on returning home at night,

There is no large Belgian town in which a chime of
bells, perched in the belfry, does not every quarter
of an hour amuse the artizan in his shop and the
trader at his counter with the peculiar harmonies of
their sonorous metal. In like manner their city halls,
their house-fronts, even their old drinking-cups are,
through their complex ornamentation, their intricate
lines and their original and often fantastic design,
agreeable to the eye. Add to this the free or well-
composed tones of the bricks forming the walls, and
the richness of the brown and red tints relieving on
white displayed on the roofs and façades—assuredly
the towns of the Netherlands are as picturesque of
their kind as any in Italy. In all times they have
delighted in *kermesses* and *fêtes de Gayant,* in corporation processions, and in the parade and glitter of
costumes and materials. I shall show you the completely Italian pomp of the civic entries and other
ceremonies in the fifteenth and sixteenth centuries.
They are epicureans as well as gourmands in the
matter of comfortable living; regularly, calmly,
without heat or enthusiasm they glean up every
pleasing harmony of savor, sound, color and form

that arises out of their prosperity and abundance, like tulips on a heap of compost. All this produces good sense somewhat limited, and happiness somewhat gross. A Frenchman would soon yawn over it, but he would make a mistake, for this civilization, which seems to him unctuous and vulgar, possesses one sterling merit—it is healthy; the men living here have a gift we lack the most—wisdom, and a compensation we are equally undeserving of—contentment.

III.

Such, in this country, is the human plant; we have now to examine its art, which is the flower. Among all the branches of the Germanic trunk, this plant alone has produced a complete flower; the art which developes so happily and so naturally in the Netherlands proves abortive with the other Germanic nations for the reason that this glorious privilege emanates from the national character as we have just set it forth.

To comprehend and love painting requires an eye sensitive to forms and to colors, and, without education or apprenticeship, one which takes pleasure in the juxtaposition of tones and is delicate in the matter of optical sensations; the man who would be a painter must be capable of losing himself in viewing the rich consonance of red and green, in watching the diminution of light as it is transformed into darkness, and in detecting the subtle hues of silks and satins, which according to their breaks, recesses and depths of fold, assume opaline tints, vague luminous gleams and imperceptible shades of blue. The eye is epicurean like the palate, and painting is an exquisite feast served up to it. For this reason it is that Germany and England have had no great-pictorial art. In Germany the too great domination of abstract ideas has left no room for the sensuousness of the eye. Its early school, that of Cologne, instead of representing bodies, represented mystic, pious and tender souls. In vain did the great German artist of the sixteenth century, Albert Dürer, familiarize himself with the Italian masters; he retains his graceless forms, his angular folds, his ugly nudities, his dull color, his barbarous, gloomy and saddened faces; the wild imagination, the deep religious sentiment and the vague philosophic divinations which shine through his works, show an intellect to which form is inadequate. Examine the infant Christ in the Louvre, by Wohlgemuth, his master, and an Eve, by Lucas Cranach, a contemporary; you will realize that the men who executed such groups and such bodies were born for theology and not for painting. Again at the present day they esteem and enjoy the inward rather than the outward; Cornelius and the Munich masters regard the idea as principal, and exe cution as secondary; the master conceives and the pupil paints; the aim of their wholly philosophic and symbolic work is to excite the spectator to reflect on some great moral or social verity. In like manner Overbeck aims at edification and preaches sentimental asceticism; and even Knauss, again, who is such an able psychologist that his pictures form idyls and comedies. As to the English, up to the eighteenth century, they do but little more than import pictures and artists from abroad. Temperament in this country is too militant, the will too stern, the mind too utilitarian, man too case-hardened, too absorbed and too over-tasked to linger over and revel in the beautiful and delicate gradations of contours and colors. Their national painter, Hogarth, simply produced moral caricatures. Others, like Wilkie, use their pencil to render sentiments and characteristic traits visible; even in landscape they depict the spiritual element, corporeal objects serving them simply as an index or suggestion; it is even apparent in their two great landscapists, Constable and Turner, and in their two great portrait painters, Gainsborough and Reynolds. Their coloring of to-day, finally, is shockingly crude, and their drawing literal minutiæ. The Flemings and Hollanders alone have prized forms and colors for their own sake. This sentiment still persists. Proof of this is to be found in the picturesqueness of their towns and in the agreeable aspect of their homes; last year at the Universal Exposition (1867) you could see for yourselves that genuine art—painting exempt from philosophic motive and literary deviation, capable of manipulating form without servility and color without barbarisms—scarcely exists anywhere but with them and with ourselves.

Thanks to this national endowment, in the fifteenth, sixteenth and seventeenth centuries, when circumstances became favorable, they were able to maintain in the face of Italy a great school of painting. But as they were Germans their school followed the German track. What distinguishes their race from classic races is, as you have seen, a preference for substance over form, of actual verity to beautiful externals, of the real, complex, irregular and natural object to the well-ordered, pruned, refined and transformed object. This instinct, of which you remark the ascendancy in their religion and literature, has likewise controlled their art and notably their painting. "The prime significance of the Flemish school," says M. Wäagen, " proceeds from its having, through its freedom from foreign influences, revealed to us the contrast of sentiments of the Greek and the German races, the two columnar capitals of ancient and modern civilization. Whilst the Greeks sought to idealize not merely conceptions taken from the ideal world, but even portraits, by simplifying the forms and accentuating the most important features, the early Flemings on the contrary translated into portraiture the ideal personifications of the Virgin, the apostles, the prophets and the martyrs, ever striving to represent in an exact manner the petty details of nature. Whilst the Greeks expressed the details of landscape, rivers, fountains and trees under abstract forms, the Flemings strove to render them precisely as they saw them. In relation to the ideal and the tendency of the Greeks to personify everything, the Flemings created a realistic school, a school of landscape. In this respect the Germans first and the English afterwards have pursued the same course." * Run over a collection of engravings containing the works of German origin from Albert Dürer, Martin Schongauer, the Van Eycks, Holbein and Lucas of Leyden, down to Rubens, Rembrandt, Paul Potter, Jan Steen and Hogarth; if your imagination is filled with noble Italian or with elegant French forms, your eyes will be offended; you will experience some difficulty in taking the proper standpoint; you will often fancy that the artist purposely studied the ugly. The truth is he is not repelled by the trivialities and deformities of life. He does not naturally enter into the symmetrical composition, the tranquil and easy action, the beautiful proportions, the healthiness and agility of the naked figure. When the Flemings in the sixteenth century resorted to the Italian school, they only succeeded in spoiling their original style. During seventy years of patient imitation they brought forth nothing but hybrid abortions. This

---

* "Manuel de l'historie de la Peinture," Vol. 1, p. 79.

long period of failure, placed between two long periods of superiority, shows the limits and the power of their original aptitudes. They were incapable of simplifying nature; they aimed to reproduce her entire. They did not concentrate her in the nude body; they assigned equal importance to all her appearances—landscapes, edifices, animals, costumes and accessories.* They are not qualified to comprehend and prize the ideal body; they are constituted to paint and enforce the actual body.

Allowing this, we easily discern in what particulars they differ from other masters of the same race. I have described to you their national genius, so sensible and so well-balanced, exempt from lofty aspiration, limited to the present and disposed to enjoyment. Such artists will not create the melan-

---

* In this respect the verdict of Michael Angelo is very instructive. "In Flanders," he says, "they prefer to paint what are called landscapes and many figures scattered here and there. . . . . There is neither art nor reason in this, no proportion, no symmetry, no careful selection, no grandeur. . . . . If I speak so ill of Flemish painting it is not because it is wholly bad, but because it seeks to render in perfection so many objects of which one alone, through its importance, would suffice, and none is produced in a satisfactory manner." We here recognize the classic and simplifying trait of Italian genius.

choly beings in painful abstraction, weighed down
with the burden of life and obstinately resigned, of
Albert Dürer. They will not devote themselves
like the mystic painters of Cologne, or the moralist
painters of England, to the representation of spiritual traits and characters; little will they concern
themselves with the disproportion between mind
and matter. In a fertile and luxurious country,
amidst jovial customs, in the presence of placid,
honest and blooming faces they are to obtain the
models suited to their genius. They almost always
paint man in a well-to-do condition and content
with his lot. When they exalt him it is without
raising him above his terrestrial condition. The
Flemish school of the seventeenth century does no
more than expand his appetite, his lusts, his energy
and his gayety. Generally they leave him as he
is. The Dutch school confines itself to reproduc-
ing the repose of the bourgeois interior, the comforts of shop and farm, out-door sports and tavern
enjoyments, all the petty satisfactions of an orderly
and tranquil existence. Nothing could be better
adapted to painting; too much thought and emo

tion is detrimental to it. Subjects of this order conceived in such a spirit, furnish works of a rare harmony; the Greeks alone, and a few great Italian
artists have set us the example; the painters of the
Netherlands on a lower stage do as they did, they
represent man to us complete of his type, adapted
to things around him and therefore happy without
effort.

One point remains to be considered. One of the
leading merits of this art is the excellence and delicacy of its coloring. This is owing to the education
of the eye, which in Flanders and in Holland is peculiar. The country is a saturated delta like that of
the Po, while Bruges, Ghent, Antwerp, Amsterdam,
Rotterdam, Hague and Utrecht, through their rivers,
canals, sea and atmosphere resemble Venice. Here,
as at Venice, nature has made man colorist. Observe the different aspect of things according as you
are in a dry country like Provençe and the neighbor-
hood of Florence, or on a wet plain like the Netherlands. In the dry country the line predominates,
and at once attracts attention; the mountains cut
sharp against the sky, with their stories of architec

ture of a grand and noble style, all objects projecting
upward in the limpid air in varied prominence.
Here the low horizon is without interest, and the
contours of objects are softened, blended and blurred
out by the imperceptible vapor with which the atmosphere is always filled; that which predominates
is the spot. A cow pasturing, a roof in the centre
of a field, a man leaning on a parapet appear as one
tone among other tones. The object emerges; it
does not start suddenly out of its surroundings as if
punched out; you are struck by its modelling, that
is to say by the different degrees of advancing luminousness and the diverse gradations of melting color
which transforms its general tint into a relief and
gives to the eye a sensation of thickness.* You

---

* W. Burger's "Musées de la Hollande," p. 206 : " Modelling, and not
lines, is what always impresses you in the beauty of the North. Form,
in the North, does not declare itself by contour, but by relief. Nature,
in expressing herself, does not avail herself of drawing, properly so
called. Walk about an Italian town for an hour, and you will encounter
women accurately defined, whose general structure brings to mind Greek
statuary, and whose profile recalls Greek cameos. You might pass a
year in Antwerp without finding a single form suggesting the idea of
translating it by a contour, but simply by saliencies, which color only can
model. . . . . Objects never present themselves as silhouettes, but, so to
say, in full shape."

would have to pass many days in this country in order to appreciate this subordination of the line to the spot. A bluish or gray vapor is constantly rising from the canals, the rivers, the sea, and from the saturated soil; a universal haze forms a soft gauze over objects, even in the finest weather. Flying scuds, like thin, half-torn white drapery, float over the meadows night and morning. I have repeatedly stood on the quays of the Scheldt contemplating the broad, pallid and slightly rippled water, on which float the dark hulks. The river shines, and on its flat surface the hazy light reflects here and there unsteady scintillations. Clouds ascend constantly around the horizon, their pale, leaden hue and their motionless files suggesting an army of spectres, the spectres of the humid soil, like so many phantoms, always revived and bringing back the eternal showers. Towards the setting sun they become ruddy, while their corpulent masses, trellissed all over with gold, remind one of the damascene copes, the brocaded simarres and the embroidered silks with which Jordaens and Rubens envelope their bleeding martyrs and their sorrowful madonnas. Quite low down

on the sky the sun seems an enormous blaze subsiding
into smoke.   On reaching Amsterdam or Ostend the
impression again deepens; both sea and sky have no
form; the fog and interposed showers leave nothing
to remember but colors.   The water changes in hue
every half hour—now of a pale wine tinge, now of a
chalky whiteness, now yellow like softened mortar,
now black like liquid soot, and sometimes of a sombre purple striped with dashes of green.   After a
few days' experience you find that, in such a nature
only gradations, contrasts and harmonies, in short,
the value of tones is of any importance.

These tones, moreover, are full and rich.   A dry
country is of a dull aspect; southern France and
the whole of the mountainous portion of Italy leave
on the eye no sensation but that of a gray and
yellow checker-board.   Besides this, all the tones
of the soil and of buildings are lost in the preponderating splendor of the sky and the all-pervading
luminousness of the atmosphere.   In truth, a southern city, and a Provençe or Tuscan landscape are
simply drawings; with white paper, charcoal, and
the feeble tints of colored crayons you can express

the whole thing. On the contrary, in a country of humidity like the Netherlands, the earth is green, a quantity of lively spots diversifying the uniformity of the wide prairie—sometimes it is the dark or brown color of the wet mould, again the deep red of tiles and bricks, again the white or rosy coating of the façades, again the ruddy spots of reclining cattle, again the flickering sheen of canals and streams. And these spots are not subdued by the too powerful light of the sky. Contrary to the dry country it is not the sky but the earth which has a preponderating influence. In Holland especially, for several months, " there is no transparency of atmosphere; a kind of opaque vail hovering between sky and ground intercepts all radiance. In winter darkness seems to come from above." * The rich colors, accordingly, with which all terrestrial objects are clothed, remain unrivalled. To their strength must be added their gradation and their mobility. In Italy a tone remains fixed; the steady light of the sky maintains it so for many hours, and as it was yesterday so it will be to-morrow. Return to it and

---

* W. Burger's 'Musées de la Hollande," p. 213.

4

you will find it the same as you placed it on your
palette a month before. In Flanders it varies incessantly along with the variations of light and the am-
bient vapor. Here again, I should like to take you
into the country and let you appreciate yourselves
the original beauty of the towns and the landscape.
The red of the bricks, the lustrous white of the
façades are agreeable to the eye because they are
softened by the grayish atmosphere; against the neu-
tral background of the sky extend rows of peaked,
shell-like roofs, all of deep brown, here and there a
gothic gutter, or some gigantic belfry covered with
elaborate finials and heraldic animals. Frequently
the crenelated cornice of chimney and of ridge is
reflected as it glows in a canal or in an arm of the
sea. Outside the cities, as within them, all is
material for pictures—you have nothing to do but
to copy. The universal green of the country is neither crude nor monotonous; it is tinted by diverse
degrees of maturity of foliage and herbage and by
the various densities and perpetual changes of hazi-
ness and clouds. It has for complement or for relief
the blackness of clouds which suddenly melt away

in transient showers, the grayness of scattered and ragged banks of fog, the vague, bluish network enveloping distances, the sparkling of flickering light arrested in flying scuds—sometimes the dazzling satin of a motionless cloud, or some abrupt opening through which the azure penetrates. A sky which is thus filled up, thus mobile, thus adapted to harmonizing, varying and emphasizing the tones of the earth, affords a colorist school. Here, as at Venice, art has followed nature, the hand having been forcibly guided by optical sensations.

If, however, the analogies of climate have endowed the Venetian eye and that of the inhabitant of the Netherlands with an analogous education, differences of climate have given them a different education. The Netherlands are situated three hundred leagues to the north of Venice. The atmosphere there is colder, rains more frequent, and the sun the oftenest concealed. Hence a natural gamut of colors, which has provoked a corresponding artificial gamut. A full light being rare, objects do not reflect the imprint of the sun. You do not meet with those golden tones, that magnificent ruddiness so frequent in the

monuments of Italy. The water is not of that deep
sea-green resembling silkiness, as in the lagoons of
Venice. The fields and trees have not that solid and
vigorous tone visible in the verdure of Verona and
Padua. The herbage is pale and softened, the water
dull or dark, the flesh white, now pink like a flower
grown in the shade, now rubicund after exposure to
the weather and rendered coarse by food, generally
yellow and flabby, sometimes, in Holland, pallid and
inanimate and of a waxy tone. The tissues of the
living organism, whether man, animal or plant, im-
bibe too much fluid, and lack the ripening power of
sunshine. This is why, if we compare the two schools
of painting, we find a difference in the general tone.
Examine, in any gallery, the Venetian school, and
afterwards the Flemish school; pass from Canaletto
and Guardi to Ruysdael, Paul Potter, Hobbema,
Adrian Van der Velde, Teniers and Ostade; from
Titian and Veronese to Rubens, Van Dyck and Rembrandt, and consult your optical impressions. On
going from the former to the latter, color loses a portion of its warmth. Shadowed, ruddy and autumnal
tones disappear; you see the fiery furnace envelop-

ing the Assumptions going out; flesh becomes of the whiteness of milk or snow, the deep purple of draperies grows lighter, and paler silks have cooler reflections. The intense brown which faintly impregnates foliage, the powerful reds gilding sunlit distances, the tones of veined marble, amethyst and sapphire with which water is resplendent, all decline, in order to give place to the deadened whiteness of expanded vapor, the bluish glow of misty twilight, the slaty reflections of the ocean, the turbid hue of rivers, the pallid verdure of the fields, and the grayish atmosphere of household interiors.

Between these new tones there is established a new harmony. Sometimes a full light falls upon objects, and to which they are not accustomed; the green campagna, the red roofs, the polished façades and the satiny flesh flushed with blood show extraordinary brilliancy. They are adapted to the subdued light of a northerly and humid country; they have not been transformed as at Venice by the slow scorching of the sun; beneath this irruption of luminousness their tones become too vivid, almost crude; they vibrate together like the blasts of trumpets,

leaving on the mind and senses an impression of
energetic and boisterous joyousness. Such is the
coloring of the Flemish painters who love the full
light of day. Rubens furnishes us with the best
example; if his restored canvasses in the Louvre
represent his work to us as it left his hands, it is certain that he did not discipline his eyes; in any event
his color lacks the rich and mellow harmony of the
Venetian; the greatest extremes meet; the snowy
whiteness of flesh, the sanguine red of the draperies,
the dazzling lustre of silks have their full force and
are not united, tempered and enveloped, as at Venice, in that amber tint which prevents contrasts from
being discordant and effects from being too startling.
Sometimes, on the contrary, the light is feeble or
nearly gone, which is commonly the case, and especially in Holland. Objects issue painfully out of
shadow; they are almost lost in their surroundings;
at evening, in a cellar, beneath a lamp, in an apartment into which a dying ray from a window glides,
they are effaced and seem to be only more intense
darks in a universal duskiness. The eye is led to
noticing these gradations of obscurity, this vague

train of light mingling with shadow, the remains of brightness clinging to the lingering lustre of the furniture, a reflection from a greenish window-sash, a piece of embroidery, a pearl, some golden spark astray upon a necklace. Having become sensitive to these delicacies, the painter, instead of uniting the extremes of the gamut, simply selects the beginning of it; his entire picture, except in one point, is in shadow; the concert he offers us is a continuous sordine in which now and then occurs some brilliant passage. He thus discloses unknown harmonies, those of chiaroscuro, those of modeling, those of emotion, all of them infinite and penetrating; using a daub of dirty yellow, or of wine lees, or a mixed gray, or vague darks, here and there accentuated by a vivid spot, he succeeds in stirring the very depths of our nature. Herein consists the last great picturesque creation; it is through this that painting nowadays most powerfully addresses the modern mind, and this is the coloring with which the light of Holland supplied the genius of Rembrandt.

You have seen the seed, the plant and the flower. A race with a genius totally opposed to that of the

Latin peoples makes for itself, after and alongside of them its place in the world. Among the numerous nations of this race, one there is in which a special territory and climate develope a particular character predisposing it to art and to a certain phase of art. Painting is born with it, lasts, becomes complete, and the physical *milieu* surrounding it, like the national genius which founds it, give to and impose upon it its subjects, its types and its coloring. Such are the remote preparatives, the profound causes, the general conditions which have nourished this sap, directed this vegetation, and produced the final efflorescence. It only remains to us now to expose historical events, the diversity and succession of which have brought about the successive and diverse phases of the great flowering epoch.

PART II.

HISTORIC EPOCHS.

I.

WE find four distinct periods in the pictorial art of the Netherlands, and, through a remarkable coincidence, each corresponds to a distinct historic period. Here, as everywhere, art translates life; the talent and taste of the painter change at the same time and in the same sense as the habits and sentiments of the public. Just as each profound geological revolution brings with it its own fauna and flora, so does each great transformation of society and intellect bring with it its ideal figures. In this respect our galleries of art resemble museums, the imaginary creations they contain being, like living organisms, both the fruit and the index of their surroundings.

The first period of art lasts about a century and a half, and extends from Hubert Van Eyck to Quintin Matsys (1400–1530). It issues from a renaissance, that is to say, from a great development of prosperity, wealth and intellect. Here, as in Italy, the cities at an early period are flourishing, and almost free. I have already stated to you that in the thirteenth century serfdom was abolished in Flanders, and that the guilds to manufacture salt "for the purpose of bringing under cultivation marshy grounds," ascend to the Roman epoch. From the seventh and ninth centuries, Bruges, Antwerp and Ghent are "ports," or privileged markets; they carry on commerce on a large scale; they fit out cruisers for the whale fishery; they serve as the entrepôts of the North and the South. Prosperous people, well supplied with arms and provisions, accustomed through association and activity to foresight and enterprise, are better qualified to protect themselves than miserable serfs scattered about in defenceless villages. Their great populous cities with narrow streets, and a saturated soil intersected with deep canals, are not a suitable ground for the cavalry of barons.* Hence it is that the feudal net, so close and so tightly drawn over all Europe, had, in Flanders, to enlarge its meshes. In vain did the Count appeal for aid to his suzerain, the French king, and urge his Burgun dian chivalry against the cities; overcome at Monsen-Puelle, at Cassel, at Rosebecque, at Othée, at

* Battle of Courtenay, 1302.

Gavre, at Brusthem, at Liege, they always recover themselves, and from revolt to revolt preserve the best portion of their liberties, even under the princes of the house of Austria. The fourteenth century is the heroic and tragic epoch of Flanders. She possesses brewers like Arteveldt, who are tribunes, dictators and captains, and who end life on the field of battle or are assassinated; civil war is mixed up with foreign war; people fight from city to city, trade against trade, and man to man; there are fourteen hundred murders in Ghent in one year; the stores of energy are so great that she survives all ills and sustains all efforts. Men seek death twenty thousand at a time, and fall in heaps before lances without giving an inch. "Banish all hope of returning without honor," said the citizens of Ghent to the five thousand volunteers under Philip Van Arteveldt, for "so soon that we hear that you are dead or discomfited we shall fire the city and destroy ourselves with our own hands."* In 1384, in the country of the Four Trades, prisoners refused their lives, declaring that after death their bones would rise up against

---

* Froissart.

the French. Fifty years later, around rebellious Ghent, the peasantry "chose death rather than ask quarter, declaring that they would perish as martyrs in a fair fight." In these swarming hives an abundance of food and habits of personal activity maintain courage, turbulence, audacity and even insolence, all excesses of brutal and boundless energy; these weavers were men, and when we encounter man we may expect soon to encounter the arts.

An interval of prosperity at this time was sufficient; under this ray of sunshine the flowering thus maturing is perfected. At the end of the fourteenth century Flanders, with Italy, is the most industrious, the wealthiest and most flourishing country in Europe.* In 1370 there are thirty-two hundred woollen factories at Malines and on its territory. One of its merchants carries on an immense trade with Damascus and Alexandria. Another, of Valenciennes, being at Paris during the fair, monopolizes all provisions exposed for sale with a view to display his opulence. Ghent in 1389 has one hundred and eighty-nine thousand men bearing arms; the

---

* Michiel's " Historie de la Peinture Flamande," Vol. II. p. 3.

drapers alone furnish eighteen thousand men in a
revolt; the weavers form twenty-seven sections, and
at the sound of the great bell, fifty-two corporations
under their own banners rush to the market-place.
In 1380 the goldsmiths of Bruges are numerous
enough to form in war time an entire division of the
army. A little later Œnius Sylvius states that she is
one of the three most beautiful cities in the world;
a canal four leagues and a half in length joins her to
the sea; a hundred vessels a day pass through it.
Bruges was then what London is at the present
time. Political matters at this period attain to a
sort of equilibrium. The Duke of Burgundy finds
himself by inheritance, in 1384, sovereign of Flanders. The grandeur of his possessions and the multiplication of civil wars during the minority and
madness of Charles VI. divorce him from France;
he is no longer, like the ancient counts, a dependant
of the king, domiciliated in Paris and soliciting
aid to reduce and tax his Flemish merchants. His
power and the misfortunes of France render him
independent. Although a prince he belongs, in
Paris, to the popular party, and the butchers shout

for him.   Although a Frenchman his politics are
Flemish, and when not in alliance with the English
he negotiates with them.   In the matter of money
he certainly quarrels with his Flemings more than
once, and is obliged to kill a good many of them.
But to one who is familiar with the disturbances and
violence of the middle ages, the order and harmony
which is then established seem sufficient; at all
events they are greater than ever before.   Henceforth, as at Florence about the year 1400, authority
becomes recognized and society organized; henceforth, as in Italy about the year 1400, man aban-
dons the ascetic and ecclesiastic regime that he may
interest himself in nature and enjoy life.   The ancient
compression is relaxed; he begins to prize strength,
health, beauty and pleasure.   On all sides we see the
mediæval spirit undergoing change and disintegra-
tion.   An elegant and refined architecture converts
stone into lace, festooning churches with pinnacles,
trefoils and intricate mullions, and in such a fashion
that the honey-combed, gilded and flowering edifice
becomes a vast and romantic casket, a product of
fancy rather than of faith, less calculated to excite

piety than wonder. In like manner chivalry becomes a mere parade. The nobles frequent the Valois court, devote themselves to pleasure, to " pretty conceits " and especially to the " conceits of love." In Chaucer and in Froissart we are spectators of their pomp — their tourneys, their processions and their banquets, of the new reign of frivolity and fashion, of the creations of an infatuated and licentious imagination, of their extravagant and overcharged costumes—robes twelve ells long, tight hose and Bohemian jackets with sleeves falling to the ground, shoes terminating in the claws, horns and tail of the scorpion, suits embroidered with letters, animals, and with musical notes enabling one to read and sing a song on the owner's back, hoods adorned with golden garlands and with animals, robes covered with sapphires, rubies and jewelled swallows, each holding in its beak a golden cup ; one costume has fourteen hundred of these cups, and we find nine hundred and sixty pearls used in embroidering a song on a coat. Women in magnificently ornamented veils, the breast nude, the head crowned with huge cones and crescents, and dressed in gaudy robes covered with the figures of unicorns, lions and savages, place themselves on seats representing small sculptured and gilded cathedrals. The life of the court and of princes seems a carnival. When Charles VI. is knighted a hall is prepared in the abbey of St. Denis, thirty-two toises (about two hundred feet) long, hung in white and green, with a lofty pavilion of tapestry: here, after three days of feasting and jousting, a nocturnal masked ball ends in an orgie. "Many a damsel forgot herself, many were the husbands who suffered," and, in contrast to this, showing the sentiments of the age, they celebrate the funeral of Duguesclin at the end of it. In the accounts and chronicles of the period we follow the course of a broad, golden stream, flowing, glistening, ostentatious and interminable, that is to say, the domestic history of the king and queen and the dukes of Orleans and Burgundy; there is nothing but entries into cities, cavalcades, masks, dances, voluptuous caprices, and the prodigality of the newly enriched. The Burgundian and French chevaliers who go to contend with Bagazet at Nicopolis equip themselves as if for a party of pleasure; their banners and the trappings of their horses are loaded with gold and silver, their dishes are all of silver plate and their tents are of green satin; exquisite wines follow them in boats on the Danube, and their camps are filled with courtesans. This excess of animal spirits, which, in France, is mingled with morbid curiosity and lugubrious fancies, breaks out in Burgundy into a grand and jolly *kermesse.* Philip the Good has three legitimate wives, twenty-four mistresses, and sixteen bastards; he attends to all, feasting, making merry and admitting the towns-women to his court; seeming at the outset to be one of Jordaens' characters. A Count of Clèves has sixty-three bastards; the chroniclers in their narration of ceremonies constantly and gravely mention those of both sexes; the institution appears to be official: seeing them swarming in this manner, we are reminded of the buxom nurses of Rubens and the Gangamelles of Rabelais. "It was," says a contemporary, "a great pity, this sin of luxury which prevailed far and wide, and especially amongst princes and the wedded. . . He was the gentlest companion who was able to deceive and possess at the

same time more than one woman . . . and even there
prevailed likewise the sin of luxury among the prel-
ates of the Church and among all Church people."*
Jacques de Croy, archbishop of Cambray, officiated
pontifically with his thirty-six bastards and bastards' sons, and kept in reserve a sum of money for
those to come. At the third marriage of Philip the
Good the gala seems to be a Gamache's wedding
commanded by Gargantua; the streets of Bruges
were hung with tapestry; for eight days and eight
nights a stone lion spurted Rhine wine, while a stone
stag discharged Beaune Burgundy; at meal times
an unicorn poured forth rosewater or malvoisie. On
the entry of the Dauphin into the city, eight hundred merchants of divers nations advanced to meet
him, all in garments of silk and velvet. At another
ceremonial the duke appears with a saddle and bri-
dle covered with precious stones; "nine pages covered with plumes of jewels" followed behind him,

---

* "C'était grand' pitié que le péché de luxare qui regnait moult et
fort, et par especial esprinces ét gens mariés. Et était le plus gentil
compagnon qui plus d'une femme savait tromper et avoir au moment . . .
et même regnait icelui péché de luxure es prélats de l'Eglise et en tous
gens d'Eglise."

and "one of the said pages bore a salad which was stated to be of the value of one hundred thousand gold crowns." Another time the jewels worn by the duke are estimated at a million. I wish to describe one of these fêtes to you; like those of Florence at the same epoch they bear witness to the picturesque and decorative tastes which here as in Florence produced pictorial art. One of them took place at Lille under Philip the Good, the Festival of the Pheasant, which may be compared with the triumph of Lorenzo de Medici; you will observe here in a hundred naive details the resemblances and the differences of the two societies, and accordingly of their culture, their taste and their art.

The Duke of Clèves had given a "superb banquet" at Lille, at which were present "Monseigneur," (of Burgundy) "together with the lords, ladies and damsels of his house." At this banquet there was seen on the table an "entremets," that is to say, a decoration representing "a ship with lifted sails, in which was a knight erect and armed . . . . and before it a silver swan, bearing on his neck a gold collar, to which hung a long chain, with which the said swan appeared to draw the vessel, and on the back of the said vessel stood a castle most skilfully contrived." On this allegorical machine the Duke of Clèves, Knight of the Swan, and "slave of the fair," caused proclamation to be made that he might be encountered in the lists, "armed in jousting harness and in war saddle, and that he who should do the best would gain a rich golden swan, chained with a chain of gold, and on the end of this chain a magnificent ruby."

Ten days after this the Count d'Etampes gave the second act of the fairy spectacle. Bear in mind that the second as well as the first act with all the others began with a feast. In this court life is gross, and people never tire of bumpers. "When the 'entremets' were removed there issued from an apartment a multitude of torches, and after these there appeared an armed attendant clad in his coat of mail, and after him two knights clad in long velvet robes furred with sable, with no covering to the head, each one bearing in his hand a gay hood of flowers;" after them, on a palfrey caparisoned in blue silk, "a most beautiful lady appeared, young, of the age of twelve years, attired in a robe of violet silk, richly embroidered and padded with gold," she is "the princess of joy." Three squires clothed in vermilion silk lead her up to the duke, singing a song as they introduce her. She descends, and kneeling on the table she places on his brow a crown of flowers. At this moment the joust is proclaimed, the drums beat, a pursuivant-at-arms appears in a mailed suit covered with swans, and then enters the Duke of Clèves, Knight of the Swan, richly armed, seated on a horse caparisoned in white damask and fringed with gold; he leads by a gold chain a large swan accompanied by two mounted archers; behind him march children on horseback, grooms, knights armed with lances, all, like himself, in white damask fringed with gold. Toison d'Or, the herald, presents them to the duchess. The other knights then defile before her on their horses, decked with gray and crimson cloth of gold, cloth decked with small golden bells, crimson velvet trimmed with sable, violet velvet fringed with gold and silk, and black velvet studded with golden tear-drops. Suppose that the great personages of state of the present day should amuse themselves with dressing up like actors at the opera and in making passes like circus-riders! The oddity of such a supposition enables you to appreciate the liveliness of the picturesque instinct at that day, as well as the taste for outward display and the feebleness of both at present.

These, however, were only preludes. Eight days after the tourney the Duke of Burgundy gave his festival, which surpassed all the others. A vast hall, hung with tapestry representing the career of Hercules, had five doors, guarded by archers dressed in robes of gray and black cloth. Around the sides extended five platforms or galleries, occupied by foreign spectators, noble personages and ladies, most of these being disguised. In their midst arose "a lofty buffet, loaded with vessels of gold and silver, and crystal vases garnished with gold and precious stones." And erect, in the centre of the hall, stood a great pillar, bearing "a female image with hair falling to her loins, her head covered with a very rich hat, and her breast spouting hypocras so long as the supper lasted." Three gigantic tables were arranged, each one being adorned with several "entremets," so many huge machines reminding one, on a grand

scale, of the toy presents given nowadays to the
children of the wealthy. The men of this time, indeed, in curiosity and in flights of the imagination
are nothing but children; their strongest desire is
to amuse the eye; they sport with life as with a
magic lantern. The two principal "entremets" consist of a monstrous pie, containing twenty-eight persons, "alive," playing on musical instruments, also a
"church with windows and glass, provided with four
choristers and a ringing bell." Besides these there
were twenty more,—a great castle, its fosses filled
with orange-water, and on a tower the fairy Melu-
sina; a windmill with archers and cross-bowmen fir-
ing at mark; a cask in a vineyard with two fluids,
one bitter and the other sweet; a vast desert with a
lion and serpent contending; a savage on a camel; a
clown prancing on a bear amidst rocks and glaciers;
a lake surrounded by cities and castles; a carrack at
anchor, bearing rigging, masts and seamen; a beautiful fountain of earth and lead, with small trees of
glass in leaf and blooming, and a St. Andrew with
his cross; a fountain of rose-water, representing a
naked infant in the attitude of the "Mannekenpiss"

5

of Brussels. You would imagine yourself in a var-
iety store at New Year time. This pêle-mêle of motionless decoration did not suffice; over and above
this an active parade was necessary; we see defiling
in turn a dozen of interludes, and in the intervals the
church and the pie keep busy the ears at the same
time as the eyes of the guests; the bell rings with
all its might; a shepherd plays on a bag-pipe; little
children sing a song; organs, German cornets, trumpets, glees, flutes, a lute with voices, drums, hunting
horns and the yelping of hounds succeed each other.
Meanwhile a rearing horse appears, richly covered
with vermilion silk, mounted by two trumpeters,
" seated backward and without saddle," led by sixteen knights in long robes; then a hobgoblin, half
man, half griffon, who, mounted on a boar and carrying a man, advances with a target and two darts;
then a large white mechanical stag, harnessed in
silk, with golden horns, and bearing on his back a
child in a short dress of crimson velvet, who sings
while the stag performs the bass. All these figures
make the circuit of the table, while the last invention
especially delights the company. A flying dragon

passes through the air, his fiery scales lighting up the recesses of the gothic ceiling. A heron and two falcons are loosed, and the vanquished bird is presented to the Duke. Trumpets sound a blast behind a curtain, which curtain being withdrawn discloses Jason reading a letter from Medea, then combating the bulls, then killing the serpent, then ploughing the ground and sowing the monster's teeth from which arises a crop of armed men. At this point the interest of the fête deepens. It becomes a romance of chivalry, a scene from Amadis, or one of Don Quixote's dreams in action. A giant arrives bearing a pike and turban and leading an elephant caparisoned in silk with a castle on his back, and in this castle a lady attired as a nun and representing the Holy Church; she orders a halt, proclaims her name, and summons the company to the crusade. Thereupon Toison d'Or, with his officers of arms, fetches a live pheasant wearing a golden collar decked with precious stones; the Duke swears upon the pheasant to succor Christendom against the Turk, and all the knights do likewise, each in a document of the style of Galaor, and this is the

pheasant's vow. The fête terminates with a mystic
and moral ball. At the sound of instruments and
by the light of torches a lady in white, bearing the
name of the " Grace of God " on her shoulder, approaches the Duke, recites a stanza and, on retir-
ing, leaves with him the twelve virtues—Faith,
Charity, Justice, Reason, Temperance, Strength,
Truth, Liberality, Diligence, Hope and Valor—each
led by a knight in a crimson pourpoint, the sleeves
of which are of satin embroidered with foliage and
jewelry. They betake themselves to dancing with
their knights, crowning the Count of Charolais the
victor in the lists, and, upon the announcement of
a new tourney, the ball ends at three o'clock in the
morning. Really there is too much of it; the mind
and the senses both flag; these people in the
way of diversions are gluttons and not epicureans.
This uproar and this profusion of quaint conceits
shows us a rude society, a race of the North, an
incipient civilization still infantile and barbarous;
the grandeur and simplicity of Italian taste is
wanting in these contemporaries of the Medicis.
And yet the groundwork of their habits and imag-

ination is the same; here, as with the chariots and
pomp of the Florentine carnival, the legends, history and philosophy of the middle ages take shape;
moral abstractions assume visible form; the virtues become actual women; they are accordingly
tempted to paint and sculpture them; all decoration,
in effect, consists of reliefs and paintings. The
symbolic age gives way to the picturesque age;
the intellect is no longer content with a scholastic
entity; it seeks to contemplate a living form, the
human mind finding it necessary for its complete-
ness to be translated to the eye by a work of art.

But this work of art bears no resemblance to that
of Italy for the reason that the culture and direction
of the intellect are different; this is evident in reading the simple and dull verses recited by the "Holy
Church" and the "Virtues," an empty, senile poetry,
the worn-out babble of the trouvères, a rattle of
rhymed phrases in which the rythm is as flimsy as
the idea. The Netherlands never had a Dante, a
Petrarch, a Boccaccio, a Villani. The mind, less
precocious and further removed from Latin traditions, remained a longer time subject to mediæval

discipline and inertia. There were no sceptical Averrhöeists and physicians like those described by Petrarch; there were no humanist restorers of ancient literature, almost pagans, like those who surrounded Lorenzo de Medici. Christian faith and sentiment are much more active and tenacious here than in Venice or in Florence. They continue to subsist under the sensual pomp of the Burgundian court. If there are epicureans in social matters there are none in theory; the most gallant serve religion, as the ladies, through a principle of honor. In 1396 seven hundred seigniors of Burgundy and France enlist in the crusade; all, save twenty-seven die at Nicopolis, and Boucicaut calls them " blessed and happy martyrs." You have just witnessed the buffoonery of Lille which ended in a solemn vow to war with the infidels. Here and there scattered traits show the persistency of the primitive devotion. In 1477, in the neighboring town of Nuremburg, Martin Kœtzel, a pilgrim in Palestine, counts the steps between Golgotha and the house of Pilate, that he may, on his return, build seven stations and a calvary between his own house and the cemetery of his

native town ; losing his measure he repeats the jour-
ney, and this time has the work executed by the
sculptor, Adam Kraft. In the Low Countries, as in
Germany, the middle class, a sedate and somewhat
dull people, restricted to their own narrow circle and
attached to ancient usages, preserve much better
than court-seigniors the faith and the fervor of the
middle ages. Their literature bears witness to this.
The moment it takes an original turn, that is to say
from the end of the thirteenth century, it furnishes
ample testimony to the practical, civic and bourgeois
spirit, with abundant evidences of pious fervor ; on
the one hand appear moral maxims, pictures of domestic life, and historic and political poems relating
to recent and true occurences ; on the other, lyric
laudation of the Virgin, and mystic and tender poetic
effusions.* In fine, the national genius, which is
Germanic, inclines much more to faith than to incre-
dulity. Through the Lollards and the mystics of
the middle ages, also through the iconoclasts and
the innumerable martyrs of the sixteenth century, it
turns in the direction of Protestant ideas. Left to

---

* Horæ Belgicæ.

itself it would have developed not, as in Italy, into a pagan renaissance, but, as in Germany, into a recrudescence of Christianity. The art, moreover, which, of all the others, best reveals the cravings of the popular imagination, architecture, remains gothic and Christian up to the end of the sixteenth century; Italian and classic importations do not affect it; the style gets to be complicated and effeminate, but the art does not change. It prevails not only in the churches but in laic edifices; the town-halls of Bruges, Louvain, Brussels, Liege and Audenarde show to what extent it was cherished not only by the priesthood but by the nation; the people remained faithful to it to the end: the town-hall of Audenarde was begun seven years after the death of Raphael. In 1536, in the hands of a Flemish woman, Margaret of Austria, the church of Brou, the latest and prettiest flower of gothic art, bloomed out in its perfection. Sum up all these indications and consider, in the protraiture of the day, the personages themselves,* the donors, abbés,

---

* See in the Musées of Antwerp, Brussels and Bruges, the triptychs whose doors present entire families of the period.

burgomasters, townspeople and matrons, so grave and so simple in their Sunday clothes and spotless linen, with their rigid air and their expression of deep and settled faith, and you will recognize that here the sixteenth century renaissance took place within religious limits, that man in making the present life more attractive never lost sight of that to come, and that his picturesque invention is the manifestation of a vivacious Christianity instead of expressing, as in Italy, a restored paganism.

A Flemish renaissance underneath Christian ideas, such, in effect, is the two-fold nature of art under Hubert and John Van Eyck, Roger Van der Weyde, Hemling and Quintin Matsys; and from these two characteristics proceed all the others. On the one hand, artists take interest in actual life; their figures are no longer symbols like the illuminations of ancient missals, nor purified spirits like the Madonnas of the school of Cologne, but living beings and bodies. They attend to anatomy, the perspective is exact, the minutest details are rendered of stuffs, of architecture, of accessories and of landscape; the relief is strong, and the entire scene stamps itself on

5*

the eye and on the mind with extraordinary force and sense of stability; the greatest masters of coming times are not to surpass them in all this, nor even go so far. Nature evidently is now discovered by them. The scales fall from their eyes; they have just mastered, almost in a flash, the proportions, the structure and the coloring of visible realities; and moreover, they delight in them. Consider the superb copes wrought in gold and decked with diamonds, the embroidered silks, the flowered and dazzling diadems with which they ornament their saints and divine personages,* all of which represents the pomp of the Burgundian court. Look at the calm and transparent water, the bright meadows, the red and white flowers, the blooming trees, the sunny distances of their admirable landscapes.† Observe their coloring—the strongest and richest ever seen, the pure and full tones side by side as in a Persian carpet, and united solely through their harmony, the

---

* " God the Father, and the Virgin," by Hubert van Eyck. '· The Virgin, St. Barbara and St. Catherine," by Memling, and "The Entombment," by Quintin Matsys.

† " St. Christopher," " The Baptism of Jesus," by Memling and his school. " The Adoration of the Lamb," by the Van Eycks.

superb breaks in the folds of purple mantles, the
azure recesses of long falling robes, the green draperies like a summer field permeated with sunshine,
the display of gold skirts trimmed with black, the
strong light which warms and enlivens the whole
scene; you have a concert in which each instrument
sounds its proper note, and the more true because
the more sonorous. They see the world on the
bright side and make a holiday of it, a genuine fête,
similar to those of this day, glowing under a more
bounteous sunlight and not a heavenly Jerusalem
suffused with supernatural radiance such as Fra
Angelico painted. They are Flemings, and they
stick to the earth. They copy the real with scrupulous accuracy, and all that is real—the ornaments of
armor, the polished glass of a window, the scrolls of
a carpet, the hairs of fur,* the undraped body of an
Adam and an Eve, a canon's massive, wrinkled and
obese features, a burgomaster's or soldier's broad
shoulders, projecting chin and prominent nose, the

---

* See "The Madonna and St. George," by Jan Van Eyck, the Antwerp triptych of Quintin Matsys, etc. The "Adam and Eve," of Hubert
Van Eyck at Brussels, and "The Adoration of the Lamb."

spindling shanks of a hangman, the over large head
and diminutive limbs of a child, the costumes and
furniture of the age; their entire work being a glorification of this present life. But, on the other hand,
it is a glorification of Christian belief. Not only are
their subjects almost all of a religious order, but
again they are imbued with a religious sentiment
which, in the following age, is not to be found in the
same scenes. Their best pictures represent no actual
event in sacred history but a verity of faith, a sum-
mary of doctrine. Hubert Van Eyck regards painting in the same light as Simone Memmi, or Taddeo
Gaddi, that is to say, as an exposition of higher theology; his figures and his accessories may be realistic, but they are likewise symbolic. The cathedral
in which Roger Van der Weyde portrays the seven
sacraments is at once a material church and a spiritual church; Christ appears bleeding on his cross,
while at the same time the priest is performing mass
at the altar. The chamber or portico in which John
Van Eyck and Memling place their kneeling saints
is an illusion in its detail and finish, but the Virgin
on her throne and the angels who crown her show

the believer that he is in a superior realm. A hie-
rarchical symmetry groups personages and stiffens
attitudes. With Hubert Van Eyck the eye is fixed
and the face impassible; it is the eternal immobility
of divine life; in heaven all is fulfilled and time is
no more. In other instances, as with Memling, there
is the quietude of absolute faith, the peace of mind
preserved in the cloister as in a sleeping forest, the
immaculate purity, mournful sweetness, the infinite
trust of the truly pious nun absorbed with her own
reveries, and whose large open eyes look out upon
vacancy. These paintings, in turn, are subjects for
the altar or private chapel; they do not appeal like
those of later ages to grand seigniors whose church-
going consists of mere routine, and who crave, even
in religious history, pagan pomp and the torsos of
wrestlers; they appeal to the faithful, in order to
suggest to them the form of the supernatural world
or the emotions of fervid piety, to show them the im-
mutable serenity of beatified saints and the tender
humility of the elect; Ruysbroeck, Eckart, Tauler
and Henry de Suzo, the theological mystics of Germany antecedent to Luther, might here resort. It is

a strange sight, and one which does not seem to
accord with the sensuous parade of the court and the
sumptuous entries of the cities.   We find a similar
contrast between the profound religious sentiment
of the Madonnas of Albert Dürer and the worldly
splendor of his " House of Maximilian."   The reason
is, we are in a Germanic country; the renaissance
of general prosperity and the emancipation of the
intellect which results from it here revive Christianity instead of destroying it as in a Latin country.

II.

When a great change is effected in human affairs it brings on by degrees a corresponding change in human conceptions. After the discovery of the Indies and of America, after the invention of printing and the multiplication of books, after the restoration of classic antiquity and the Reformation of Luther, any conception of the world then formed could no longer remain monastic and mystic. The tender and melancholy aspiration of a soul sighing for the celestial kingdom and humbly subjecting its conduct to the authority of an undisputed Church gave way to free inquiry nourished on so many fresh conceptions, and disappeared at the admirable spectacle of this real world which man now began to comprehend and to conquer. The rhetorical academies which, at first, were composed of a clerical body passed into the hands of the laity; they had preached the payment of tithes and submission to the Church ; they now ridiculed the clergy and combated ecclesiastical abuses.

In 1533 nine citizens of Amsterdam were condemned
to a pilgrimage to Rome for having represented one
of these satirical pieces.   In 1539, at Ghent, the
question having been proposed of : Who are the
greatest fools in the world ? eleven out of nineteen
academies reply : The monks.   " A few poor monks
and nuns," says a contemporary, " always appear in
the comedies ; it seems as if people could not enjoy
themselves without making sport of God and the
Church."   Philip II. had decreed the punishment of
death against authors and actors whose pieces were
not authorized or were impious.   But they were performed, nevertheless, even in the villages.   " The
word of God," says the same author, " first found its
way into these countries through plays, and for this
reason they are forbidden much more rigidly than
the writings of Martin Luther." *   It is evident that
the mind had become emancipated from ancient
tutelage, and that people and burghers, artizans and

* In 1539 Louvain proposes this question : " What is the greatest con-
solation to a dying man ?"   The responses all have a Lutheran cast.   The
Academy of St. Wynockberge, bearing off the second prize, answers,
according to the doctrine of pure grace : " The faith that Christ and his
Spirit have been given to us."

merchants began to think for themselves on matters of salvation and morality.

The extraordinary wealth and prosperity of the country lead to picturesque and sensuous customs; here, as in England at the same epoch, a renaissance pomp overlays a silent Protestant fermentation. When Charles V., in 1520, made his entry into the city of Antwerp, Albert Dürer saw four hundred triumphal arches, two stories high and forty feet long, decorated with paintings on which allegorical representations were given. The performers consisted of young girls belonging to the best bourgeois class, clothed simply in thin gauze, "almost naked," says the honest German artist,—"I have rarely seen more beautiful. I gazed at them very attentively, and even passionately, inasmuch as I am a painter." The festivals of the belle-lettre academies become magnificent; cities and communities rival each other in luxurious allegorical creations. At the invitation of the violinists of Antwerp fourteen academies, in 1562, send their "triumphs," and the academy called the *Guirlande de Marie*, at Brussels, obtains the prize. "For," says Van Meteren, "there were full three hundred and forty men on horseback, all dressed in velvet and in dark purple silk, with long Polish cassocks embroidered with silver lace, and wearing red hats fashioned like antique helmets; their pourpoints, plumes and bootees were white. They wore belts of silver tocque, very ingeniously woven with yellow, red, blue and white. They had seven chariots made after the antique pattern, with divers personages borne thereon. They had, beside, seventy-eight ordinary chariots with torches; the said chariots were covered with red cloth bordered with white. The charioteers all wore red mantles, and on these chariots were divers personages representing a number of beautiful antique figures, all of which goes to show how people will assemble in friendship to share in amity." *La Pione de Malines* provides a parade almost equal to this consisting of three hundred and twenty men on horseback, attired in a flesh-colored material embroidered with gold, seven antique chariots emblazoned and flaming with all sorts of lights. Add to this the entry of twelve other processions, and then enumerate the plays, pantomines, fireworks and ban-

quets which follow after. "There were several similar games given during the peace in other cities. . . . .
I have deemed it proper to narrate all this," says Van
Meteren, "for the purpose of showing the happy
union and prosperity of those countries in those
days." After the departure of Philip II., "instead of
one court there seemed to be a hundred and fifty."
The nobles vied with each other in magnificence,
maintaining free tables and spending without stint.
On one occasion the Prince of Orange, wishing to
diminish his train, discharged in a body twenty-
eight head cooks. Lordly mansions swarmed with
pages and gentlemen and superb liveries; the full
tide of the renaissance overflowed in folly and
extravagance, as under Elizabeth in England, in
pompous array, cavalcades, games and good cheer.
The Count of Brederode drank so much at one of
St. Martin's feasts that he came near dying; the
rhinegrave's brother did actually die at the table
through too great fondness of Malvoisie wine. Never
did life seem more bright or beautiful. Like Florence under the Medicis in the preceding century, it
ceased to be tragic; man had expanded; murderous

revolts and sanguinary wars between city and city and corporation and corporation quietly subsided; only one sedition takes place in Ghent in 1536 which is easily quelled without much bloodshed, the last and a feeble convulsion, not to be compared with the formidable insurrections of the fifteenth century. Margaret of Austria, Mary of Hungary, and Margaret of Parma, the three rulers, are popular; Charles V. is a national prince, speaking Flemish, boasting of his nativity in Ghent, and protecting, by treaties, the manufactures and trade of the country. He fosters and nourishes it; Flanders, in return, supplies him with the half of his entire revenue;* in his herd of states she is the fat milch cow which is milked constantly without being dried up. Thus, while the mind is expanding, the temperature around it becomes modified and establishes the conditions of a new growth; we see the dawn of it in the festivals of the belle-lettre academies, which are classic representations precisely like those of the Florence carnival and quite different from the quaint conceits accumulated at the banquets of the Dukes of Bur-

---

* Two million of crowns of gold out of five million.

gundy. "The 'Violet,' 'Olive' and 'Thought' academies of Antwerp," says Guiccardini, "give public performances of comedies, tragedies and other histories in imitation of the Greeks and Romans." Society, ideas and tastes have undergone a transformation, and there is room for a new art.

Already in the preceding epoch we see premonitory symptoms of the coming change. From Hubert Van Eyck to Quintin Matsys the grandeur and gravity of religious conceptions have diminished. Nobody now dreams of portraying the whole of Christian faith and doctrine in a single picture; scenes are selected from the Gospel and from history—annunciations, shepherd adorations, last judgments, martyrdoms and moral legends. Painting, which is epic in the hands of Hubert Van Eyck, becomes idyllic in those of Hemling and almost worldly in those of Quintin Matsys. It gets to be pathetic, interesting and pleasing. The charming saints, the beautiful Herodias and the lithe Salome of Quintin Matsys are richly attired noble dames and already laic; the artist loves the world as it is and for itself, and does not subordinate

it to the representation of the supernatural world;
he does not employ it as a means but as an end.
Scenes of profane life multiply; he paints townspeople in their shops; money - changers, amorous
couples, and the attenuated features and stealthy
smiles of a miser. Lucas of Leyden, his contemporary, is an ancestor of the painters whom we call
the lesser Flemings; his "Presentation of Christ"
and "The Magdalen's Dance" have nothing religious about them but their titles; the evangelical
subject is lost in the accessories; that which the
picture truly presents is a rural Flemish festival, or
a gathering of Flemings on an open field. Jerome
Bosch, of the same period, paints grotesque, infernal
scenes. Art, it is clear, falls from heaven to earth,
and is no longer to treat divine but human incidents.
Artists, in other respects, lack no process and no
preparation ; they understand perspective, they
know the use of oil, and are masters of modelling
and relief; they have studied actual types; they
know how to paint dresses, accessories, architecture
and landscape with wonderful accuracy and finish ;
their manipulative skill is admirable. One defect

only still chains them to hieratic art, which is the immobility of their faces and the rigid folds of their stuffs. They have but to observe the rapid play of physiognomies and the easy movement of loose drapery, and the renaissance is complete; the breeze of the age is behind them and already fills their sails. On looking at their portraits, their interiors, and even their sacred personages, as in the "Entombment" of Quintin Matsys, one is tempted to address them thus: "You are alive—one effort more! Come, bestir yourselves! Shake off the middle age entirely! Depict the modern man for us as you find him within you and outside of you. Paint him vigorous, healthy and content with existence. Forget the meagre, ascetic and pensive spirit, dreaming in the chapels of Hemling. If you choose a religious scene for the motive of your picture, compose it, like the Italians, of active and healthy figures, only let these figures proceed from your national and personal taste. You have a soul of your own, which is Flemish and not Italian; let the flower bloom; judging by the bud it will be a beautiful one." And, indeed, when we regard the

sculptures of the time, such as the chimney of the
Palais de Justice and the tomb of Charles the Bold
at Bruges, the church and monuments of Brou,
we see the promise of an original and complete art,
less sculptural and less refined than the Italian, but
more varied, more expressive and closer to nature,
less subject to rule but nearer to the real, more
capable of manifesting spirit and personality, the
impulses, the unpremeditated, the diversities, the
lights and darks of education, temperament and
age of the individual; in short, a Germanic art
which indicates remote successors to the Van Eycks
and remote predecessors of Rubens.

They never appeared, or at all events, they imper-
fectly fulfilled their task. No nation, it must be
noted, lives alone in the world; alongside of the
Flemish renaissance there existed the Italian renaissance, and the large tree stifled the small plant. It
flourished and grew for a century; the literature,
the ideas and the masterpieces of precocious Italy
imposed themselves on sluggish Europe, and the
Flemish cities, through their commerce, and the Austrian dynasty, through its possessions and its Italian

affairs, introduced into the North the tastes and models of the new civilization. Towards 1520 the Flemish painters began to borrow from the artists of Florence and Rome. John of Mabuse is the first one who, in 1513, on returning from Italy, introduced the Italian into the old style, and the rest followed. It is so natural in advancing into an unexplored country to take the path already marked out! This path, however, is not made for those who follow it; the long line of Flemish carts is to be delayed and stuck fast in the disproportionate ruts which another set of wheels have worn. There are two traits characteristic of Italian art, both of which run counter to the Flemish imagination. On the one hand Italian art centres on the natural body, healthy, active and vigorous, endowed with every athletic aptitude, that is to say, naked or semi-draped, frankly pagan, enjoying freely and nobly in full sunshine every limb, instinct and animal faculty, the same as an ancient Greek in his city or palestrum, or, as at this very epoch, a Cellini on the Italian streets and highways. Now a Fleming does not easily enter into this conception. He belongs to a cold and humid climate; a

man there in a state of nudity shivers. The human
form here does not display the fine proportions nor
the easy attitudes required by classic art; it is often
dumpy or too gross; the white, soft, yielding flesh,
easily flushed, requires to be clothed. When the
painter returns from Rome and strives to pursue Italian art, his surroundings oppose his education; his
sentiment being no longer renewed through his con-
tact with living nature, he is reduced to his souvenirs.
Moreover, he is of Germanic race; in other terms he
is organically a morally good-natured man, and even
modest; he has difficulty in appreciating the pagan
idea of nudity, and still greater difficulty in comprehending the fatal and magnificent idea* which governs civilization and stimulates the arts beyond the
Alps, namely, that of the complete and sovereign
individual, emancipated from every law, subordina-
ting the rest, men and things, to the development of
his own nature and the growth of his own faculties.
Our painter is related, although distantly, to Martin

---

* Burckhardt's "Die Cultur der Renaissance in Italien," an admirable
work, the most complete and most philosophic yet written on the Italian
Renaissance.

Schœn and Albert Dürer; he is a bourgeois, almost docile and staid, a lover of the comfortable and the decent, and adapted to family and domestic life. His biographer, Karl Van Mander, at the beginning of his book, furnishes him with moral precepts. Read this patriarchal treatise, and imagine the distance between a Rosso, a Giulio Romano, a Titian and a Giorgione, and their pupils of Leyden or Antwerp. "All vices," says the good Fleming, "bring their own punishment. Distrust the maxim that the best painter is he who is the most dissipated. Unworthy of the name of artist is he who leads an evil life. Painters should never dispute or enter into strife with each other. To squander one's property is not a meritorious art. Avoid paying court to women in your youthful days. Shun the society of frivolous women, who corrupt so many painters. Reflect before you depart for Rome, for the opportunities to spend money there are great, and none are there for earning it. Ever be thankful to God for His bounties." Special recommendations follow concerning Italian inns, bed linen and fleas. It is evident that pupils of this class, even with great labor, will produce but little more than academic figures; man, according to their conceptions, is a draped body; when, following the example of the Italian masters, they attempt the nude, they render it without freedom, without spirit, without vivacity of invention; their pictures, in fact, are simply cold and meagre imitation; their motive is pedantic; they execute servilely and badly that which, in Italy, is done naturally and well. On the other hand, Italian art, like Greek art, and, in general, all classic art, simplifies in order to embellish; it eliminates, effaces, and reduces detail; by this means it gives greater value to grander features. Michael Angelo and the admirable Florentine school subordinate or suppress accessories, landscape, fabrics and costume; with them the essential consists of the noble and the grandiose type, the anatomical and muscular structure, the nude or lightly draped form taken by itself, abstractly, through the retrenchment of particulars constituting the individual and denoting his profession, education and condition; you have man in general represented, and not a special man. Their personages are in a superior world, because they are of a world which is not; the peculiar feature of the scene they depict is the nullity of time and space. Nothing is more opposed to Germanic and Flemish genius, which sees things as they are in their entirety and complexity; which, in man, takes in, besides man in general, the contemporary, the citizen, the peasant, the laborer, this citizen, that laborer, that peasant; which attaches as much importance to the accessories of a man as to the man himself; which loves not merely human nature but all nature, animate and inanimate—cattle, horses, plants, landscape, sky, and even the atmosphere—its broader sympathies forestalling any neglect of objects, and its more minute observation requiring the fullest expression. You can comprehend how, in subjecting itself to a discipline so contrary, it loses the qualities it had without acquiring those it had not; how, in order that it may arrogate the ideal, it reduces color, loses the sentiment of light and atmosphere, obliterates the true details of costume and of interiors, deprives figures of original diversities peculiar to portrait and person, and is led to moderate the suddenness of motion constituting the impulsiveness of nature's activity,

and thereby impairing ideal symmetry. It finds
difficulty, however, in making all these sacrifices;
its instinct only partially yields to its education.
Flemish reminiscences may be traced underneath
Italian velleity; both in turn predominate in the
same picture; each prevents the other from having
their full effect; their painting, consequently, uncer-
tain, imperfect and diverted by two tendencies, fur-
nishing us with historical documents and not beautiful works of art.

Such is the spectacle presented in Flanders during the last three quarters of the sixteenth century.
Like a small river receiving a large stream, the mingled waters of which are disturbed until the foreign
affluent imposes its more powerful tint on the entire
current, so do we find the national style, invaded by
the Italian, dappled irregularly and in places, gradually disappearing, only rarely rising to the surface,
and at last sinking into obscure depths, whilst the
other displays itself in the light and attracts universal attention. It is interesting to trace in the public
galleries this conflict of the two currents and the
peculiar effects of their commingling. The first Ital-

ian influx takes place with John de Mabuse, Bernard Van Orley, Lambert Lombard, John Mostaert, John Schorel, and Launcelot Blondel. They import in their pictures classic architecture, veined marble pilasters, medallions, shell niches, sometimes triumphal arches and cariatides, sometimes also noble and vigorous female figures in antique drapery, a sound nude form, well proportioned and vitalized, of the fine pagan stock, and healthy; their imitation reduces itself to this, while in other respects they follow national traditions. They still paint small pictures, suitable for genre subjects; they almost always preserve the strong and rich coloring of the preceding age, the mountains and blue distances of John Van Eyck, the clear skies vaguely tinged with emerald on the horizon, the magnificent stuffs covered with gold and jewels, the powerful relief, the minute precision of detail, and the solid honest heads of the bourgeoisie. But as they are no longer restrained by hieratic gravity they fall, in attempting to emancipate themselves, into simple awkwardness and ridiculous inconsistencies. The children of Job, crushed by their falling palace, sprawl about grimacing and writhing as if possessed; on the other panel of the triptych is the devil in the air mounting upward like a bat towards the petty Christ of a missal. Long feet and lean ascetic hands form the odd appurtenances of a shapely body. A "Last Supper" by Lambert Lombard mingles together Flemish clumsiness and vulgarity with the composition of Da Vinci. A "Last Judgment" by Bernard Van Orley introduces demons by Martin Schœn amidst the academic figures of Raphael. In the next generation the rising flood begins to engulph all; Michael Van Coxcyen, Heemskerk, Franz Floris, Martin de Vos, the Franckens, Van Mander, Spranger, Pourbus the elder, and later, Goltzius, besides many others, resemble people ambitious of speaking Italian but who do so laboriously, with an accent and some barbarisms. The canvas is enlarged and approaches the usual dimensions of an historical subject; the manner of painting is less simple; Karl Van Mander reproaches his contemporaries with "overloading their brushes," which was not formerly done, and with carrying *impasto* to excess. Coloring dies out; it becomes more and more white, chalky and pallid. Painters enter

passionately into the study of anatomy, foreshorten-
ings and muscular development; their drawing becomes dry and hard, reminding one at once of the
goldsmiths contemporary with Pollaiolo and the ex-
aggerating disciples of Michael Angelo; they lay
great or violent stress on their science, they insist on
proving their ability to manipulate the skeleton and
produce action; you will find Adams and Eves,
Saint Sebastians, Massacres of the Innocents, and
Horatii resembling grotesque forms of living and
bare muscles; their personages look as if casting
their skins. When they show more moderation, and
the painter, like Franz Floris in his "Fall of the Angels," discreetly copies good classic models, his nudities are scarcely any better; realistic sentiment and
the quaint Germanic imagination peer out among
ideal forms; demons with the heads of cats, fishes
and swine, and with horns, claws and humps, and
blowing fire from their jaws, introduce bestial com-
edy and a fantastic sabbat into the midst of the noble
Olympus; we have one of Teniers' buffooneries in-
serted in a poem by Raphael. Others, like Martin
Vos, strain themselves to produce the great sacred

6*

picture, figures imitated from the antique, cuirasses, draperies and tunics, studied correctness in composition, gestures indicative of noble action and stage heads and head gear, while they are substantially genre painters and lovers of reality and accessories. They constantly fall back to their Flemish types and their domestic details; their pictures seem to be enlarged colored engravings; they would be much better were they of small size. We feel in the artist a perverted talent, a natural disposition thwarted, an instinct working against the grain, a prose-writer born for narrating social incidents of whom the public commands epics in sounding Alexandrines.* Still another wave, and the remains of national genius seem wholly submerged. A painter of noble family, well brought up, instructed by an erudite, a man of the world and a courtier, a favorite of the great Italian and Spanish leaders who manage matters in the Netherlands, Otto Venius, after passing seven years in Italy, brings from that country noble and pure

---

* This period of Flemish art is analogous to that of English literature after the Restoration. In both cases a Germanic art attempts to be classic; in both cases the contrast between education and nature produces hybrid works and multiplied failures.

antique types, beautiful Venetian color, melting and
subtly graduated tones, shadows permeated with
light, and the vague purples of flesh and of ruddy
foliage. Excepting his native stimulus he is Italian,
and no longer belongs to his race; scarcely more
than a fragment of costume or the simple attitude of
a stooping old man connects him with his country.
Nothing remains to the painter but to abandon it
entirely. Denis Calvaert establishes himself at Bologna, enters into competition with the Caraccis, and
is the master of Guido. Flemish art accordingly
seems, through its own course, to suppress itself for
the advantage of another.

And yet it still subsists underneath the other. In
vain does the genius of a people yield to foreign influences. It always recovers. These are temporary,
while that is eternal; it belongs to the flesh and the
blood, the atmosphere and the soil, the structure and
degree of activity of brain and senses; all are ani-
mating forces incessantly renewed and everywhere
present, and which the transient applause of a superior civilization neither undermines nor destroys.
This is apparent in the preservation of two styles

which continue pure amidst the growing transformation of the others. Mabuse, Morstaert, Van Orley, the two Pourbus, John Van Cleve, Antonis Moor, the two Mierevelts and Paul Moreelze produce excellent portraits; often, in the triptychs, the faces of the donataires, arranged in rows on the shutters, form a contrast in their homely sincerity, calm gravity and profound simplicity of expression with the frigidity and artificial composition of the principal subject; the spectator feels himself quite re-animated; instead of manikins he finds men. On the other hand there arises the painting of genre subjects, landscapes and interiors. After Quintin Matsys, and Lucas of Leyden, we see it developing with John Matsys, Van Hemessen, the Breughels, Vinckenbooms, the three Valkenburgs, Peter Neefs and Paul Bril, and especially in the multitude of engravers and illustrators who reproduce, on scattered sheets or in books, the moralities, social incidents, professions, conditions and events of the day. They are, undoubtedly, to remain for a long time fantastic and humorous. This art mixes up nature promiscuously, according to its own disordered fancies; it is unconscious of the

true forms and the true tint of trees and mountains;
it makes its figures howling, and introduces amidst
the costumes of the period grotesque monsters sim
ilar to those promenading through the *kermesses.*
But all these intermediary objects are natural, and
insensibly lead on to its final state, which is the
knowledge and love of actual life, as the eye con-
templates it. Here, as in the painting of portraits,
the chain is complete; the metal of all its links is
national; through Breughel, Paul Bril and Peter
Neefs, through Antonis Moor, the Pourbus and the
Mierevelts, it joins on to the Flemish and Dutch
masters of the seventeenth century. The rigidity of
ancient figures is relaxed; a mystic landscape becomes real; the transition from the divine to the
human age is accomplished. This spontaneous and
regular development shows that national instincts
are maintained under the empire of foreign fashions;
let a crisis intervene to arouse them, and they recover their ascendancy, while art is transformed according to the public taste. This crisis is the great
revolution commencing in 1572, the long and terrible
War of Independence, as grand in its events and as

fecund of results as our French Revolution. Here, as with us, the renewal of the moral world is the renewal of the ideal world; the Flemish and Dutch art of the seventeenth century, like the French art and literature of the nineteenth century, is the reaction of a vast tragedy performed for thirty years at the cost of hundreds of thousands of lives. Here, however, the scaffolds and battles, having divided the nation, form two peoples; one Catholic and legitimist in Belgium, and the other Protestant and republican in Holland. While both were combined there was but one spirit; divided and opposed there were two. Antwerp and Amsterdam held different conceptions of life, and, accordingly, display different schools of painting; the same political crisis which divided their country divided their art.

III.

We must look closely into the formation of Belgium* in order to comprehend the rise of the school which bears the name of Rubens. Previous to the War of Independence the Southern provinces seemed to tend to the Reformation as well as the provinces of the North. In 1566 bands of iconoclasts had devastated the cathedrals of Antwerp, Ghent and Tournay, and broken everywhere, in the churches and the abbeys, all images and ornaments deemed idolatrous. In the environs of Ghent thousands of armed Calvinists flocked to the preachings of Hermann Stricker. Crowds gathered around the stake, sang psalms, sometimes stoned the executioners and set the condemned free. Death penalties had to be enacted in order to suppress the satires of the belle-lettre academies, and when the Duke of Alba began

---

* All are aware that this name dates from the French Revolution. I employ it here as the most convenient term. The historic designation of Belgium is "The Spanish Low Countries," and of Holland "The United Provinces."

his massacres the whole country rushed to arms.
The resistance, however, was not the same in the
South as in the North; in the South the Germanic
race, the independent and Protestant race, was not
pure; the Walloons, a mixed population speaking
French, constituted one half of the inhabitants.
The soil, moreover, being richer, and living easier,
there was less energy and greater sensuality; man
was less resolved to suffer and more inclined to
enjoy.   Finally, almost all the Walloons, besides the
families of the great, being attached to court sentiment through a court life, were Catholic.   Hence it
is that the Southern provinces did not contend with
the indomitable stubbornness of the Northern provinces.   There is nothing in them like the sieges of
Maestricht, Harlem, Alkmaar and Leyden, where
women enlisted, fought, and were slaughtered in
the breach.   After the taking of Antwerp by the
Duke of Parma the ten provinces returned to their
allegiance, and began apart a new existence.   The
most spirited citizens and the most fervent Calvinists had perished in battle and on the scaffold, or had
fled to the North in the seven free provinces.   The

belle-lettre academies exiled themselves there in a body. On the termination of the Duke of Alva's administration it was estimated that sixty thousand families had emigrated; after the capture of Ghent eleven thousand more departed, and after the capitulation of Antwerp four thousand weavers betook themselves to London. Antwerp lost the half of its inhabitants, and Ghent and Bruges two-thirds; whole streets were empty; in the principal street of Ghent a couple of horses cropped the grass. A mighty surgical operation had relieved the nation of what the Spaniards called its bad blood; at all events that which remained was the most quiescent. There is a great substratum of docility in the Germanic races; think of the German regiments exported to America and sold there to die by their petty absolute princes: the sovereign once accepted, they are faithful to him; with guaranteed rights he seems legitimate; they are inclined to respect the established order of things. The continued constraint, moreover, of irremediable necessity produces its effect; man accommodates himself to things when he is satisfied that he cannot change them·

certain portions of his character which cannot be developed languish, and others expand the more. There are moments in the history of a nation when it bears some resemblance to Christ taken to the top of a high mountain by Satan, and there bid to choose between a heroic and a common life; here the tempter is Philip II., with his armies and executioners; the people of the North and the South, both subject to the same trial, decide differently according to the petty diversities of their composition and character. The choice made these diversities grow, and are exaggerated by the effects of the situation they themselves have produced. Both people being two almost indeterminate varieties of one species become two distinct species. It is with moral types as with organic types; they issue at the beginning from a common origin, but as they complete their development they grow wider apart and are thus formed through their divergencies. The Southern provinces henceforth become Belgium. The dominant trait is the craving for peace and comfort, the disposition to take life on the jovial and pleasant side, in brief, the sentiment of

Teniers. In fact, even in a dilapidated cabin or in a bare tavern on a wooden bench a man may laugh, sing, smoke a good pipe and swallow deep draughts of beer; it is not disagreeable to attend mass as a fine ceremony, nor to recount one's sins to an accommodating Jesuit. After the capture of Antwerp, Philip II. is delighted to hear that communions have become more and more frequent. Convents are founded twenty at a time. "It is a matter worthy of remark," says a contemporary, "that since the happy advent of the archdukes more new establishments have arisen than in two hundred years and before that"—Franciscans, reformed Carmelites, friars of St. Francis de Paule, Carmelites, annunciada, and especially the Jesuits; the latter in fact bring with them a new Christianity, the most appropriate to the state of the country, and which seems manufactured purposely to contrast with that of the Protestants. Be docile in mind and in heart, and all the rest is tolerance and indulgence; in this connection see the portraits of the day, and among others, the gay fellow who was confessor to Rubens. Casuistry is shaped to and serves for difficult cases;

under its empire there is scope enough for all current peccadilloes. Worship, moreover, is exempt from prudery, and winds up by being amusing. To this epoch belongs the worldly and sensualistic internal decoration of the grave and venerable cathedral, the multiplied and contorted ornaments— flames, lyres, trinkets and scrolls, the veneerings of veined marbles, altars resembling theatre façades, and the quaint diverting pulpits overlaid with a menagerie of carved birds and brutes. As respects the new churches, the outside suits the inside. That of the Jesuits, built in Antwerp at the beginning of the seventeenth century, is instructive, it being a saloon filled with *étagères*. Its thirty-six ceilings were executed by Rubens, and it is curious to see here as elsewhere an ascetic and mystic faith accept as edifying subjects the most blooming and the most exposed nudities, buxom Magdalens, plump St. Sebastians and Madonnas whom the negro magi are devouring with all the lust of their eyes, a display of flesh and fabrics unequalled by the Florentine carnival in luxurious temptation and in triumphant sensuality.

Meanwhile the altered political situation contributes to the transformation of the intellectual world. The old despotism becomes relaxed; to the rigors of the Duke of Alva succeeds the liberal policy of the Duke of Parma. After an amputation, a man who has bled profusely must be restored by soothing and strengthening treatment; hence it is that, after the pacification of Ghent, the Spaniards let their terrible edicts against heresy lie dormant. Executions are at an end. The latest martyr is a poor sewing woman, buried alive in 1597. In the following century Jordaens, with his wife and her family, become Protestants without being annoyed, and even without losing any of his commissions. The archdukes permit towns and corporations to govern themselves according to ancient usages, to collect imposts and attend to their own business; when they desire to have Breughel de Velours relieved of military duty or of exactions, they make their appeal to the commune. The government becomes regular, semi-liberal, and almost national; Spanish extortions, razzias, and brutalities disappear. At length, in order to keep possession of the country, Philip II. is compelled to let it remain Flemish, and exist as a separate state. In 1599 he detaches it from Spain, and cedes it in full possession to Albert and Isabella. "The Spaniards never did a better thing," writes the French ambassador; "it would be impossible to keep the country without giving it this new system, as it was ripe for revolution." The States-General meet in 1600, and decide for reforms. We see in Guiccardini, and other travellers, that the old constitution arises almost intact out of the rubbish under which it had been buried by military violence. "At Bruges," M. de Monconys writes in 1653, "each trade has a house in common, where those of the profession meet to transact the business of the community, or for recreation; and all the trades are distributed into four divisions, under the control of four burgomasters, who have charge of the keys of the city, the Governor exercising no jurisdiction or power over any but the military force." The archdukes are wise and solicitous of the public welfare. In 1609 they make peace with Holland; in 1611 their perpetual edict completes the restoration of the country. They either are or render themselves powerful; Isabella, with her own hand, strikes down, on the Place de Sablon, the bird which sanctifies the cross-bowman's pledge; Albert attends at Louvain the lectures of Justus Lepsius. They love, cherish, and attach themselves to famous artists—Otto Venius, Rubens, Teniers, and Breughel de Velours. The belle-lettre institutions flourish again, and the universities are favored; in the Catholic world, under the Jesuits and often by their side, is a kind of intellectual renaissance; a number of theologians, controversialists, casuists, erudites, geographers, physicians, and even historians, arise—Mercator, Ortelius, Van Helmont, Jansenius, Lepsius, all of whom are Flemings of this epoch. The "Description of Flanders," by Sander, a vast work completed after so many trials, is a monument of national zeal and patriotic pride. If, in turn, we wish to form an idea of the state of the country, take one of the tranquil and fallen cities to-day like Bruges. Sir Dudley Carleton, passing through Antwerp in 1616, finds it a handsome place, although nearly empty; he may have seen no more than "forty persons in the entire street," not a carriage, not a horseman, not a cus-

tomer in the shops; but the houses are well maintained, everything being clean and cared for: the
peasant has rebuilt his burnt cabin and is at work
in the field; the housewife is attending to her duties;
security has returned, and is about to be followed
by plenty; there are shooting matches, processions,
fairs and magnificent entries of princes; people are
getting back to old comforts beyond which they do
not aspire; religion is left to the Church, and government to the princes: here, as at Venice, the
course of events has brought man down to the quest
of enjoyment—the effort to obtain it being the more
strenuous in proportion to the strong contrast with
their previous misery.

And, in truth, what a contrast! It is necessary
to have read the details of the war in order to appreciate it. Fifty thousand martys had perished
under Charles V., eighteen thousand persons had
been executed by the Duke of Alva, and the re-
volted country had maintained the war for thirteen
years. The Spaniards had reconquered the large
cities only by famine after protracted sieges. In
the beginning Antwerp was sacked for three days;

seven thousand of her citizens were slain, and five
hundred houses were burnt. The soldier lived on
the country, and we see him in the engravings of
the day plundering and robbing dwellings, torturing
the husband, violating the wife, and bearing away
chests and furniture in carts. When his pay was
withheld too long he took up his quarters in a town,
and this led to a republic of brigands; under an
eletto of their own choice they ravaged the environs
at their convenience. Karl Van Mander, the historian of the painters, on returning one day to his
village, found his house pillaged along with the
rest; the soldiers had even taken the bed and bed-
clothes of his old sick father. Karl was driven out
naked, and they were already fixing a rope to his
neck to hang him when he was saved by a cavalier
whom he had known in Italy. Another time, as he
was on the road with his wife and an infant child,
they took his money, baggage and clothes, his wife's
and those of the infant; the mother could only
secure a small petticoat, the infant a tattered net,
and Karl an old worn-out piece of cloth in which
he wrapped himself up, and in which guise he

7

reached Bruges. Under this regime a country ceases to exist; soldiers themselves finally die of starvation; the Duke of Parma writes to Philip II. that if he fails to send relief the army is lost, "for nobody can live without eating." On emerging from such calamities, peace seems a paradise; it is not merely the *good* at which man rejoices, but the *better*, and here the better is stupendous. A man can now sleep in his own bed, store up provisions, enjoy the fruits of his labor, travel about and assemble and converse with his fellows without fear; he has a home, a country and a future. All the ordinary occurrences of life get to be interesting and attractive; he revives, and for the first time seems to live. It is circumstances like these out of which always springs a spontaneous literature and an original art. The great crisis through which the nation has passed serves to remove the monotonous varnish with which tradition and custom have overspread things. We find out what man is; we seize on the fundamental points of his renewed and transformed nature; we see its depth, its secret instincts, the master forces which denote his race and are

about to control his history; half a century later
and we see them no more, because during a half
century they have been constantly visible. In the
meantime, however, the new order of things becomes complete; the mind confronts it like Adam
on his first awakening; it is only later that conceptions get to be over-refined and weakened; they
are now broad and simple. Man is qualified for this
through his birth in a crumbling society and an
education in the midst of veritable tragedies; like
Victor Hugo and George Sand, the child Rubens, in
exile, alongside of his imprisoned father, hears, in
his home and all around him, the roar of tempest
and of wreck. After an active generation which
has suffered and created, comes the poetic generation which writes, paints or models. It expresses
and amplifies the energies and desires of a society
founded by its fathers. Hence it is that Flemish
art proceeds to glorify in heroic types the sensual
instincts, the grand and gross joyousness, the rude
energy of surrounding mortals, and to find in the
alehouse of Teniers the Olympus of Rubens.

Among these painters there is one who seems to

efface the rest; indeed no name in the history of art is greater, and there are only three or four as great. But Rubens is not an isolated genius, the number as well as the resemblance of surrounding talents showing that the efflorescence of which he is the most beautiful emanation is the product of his time and people. Before him there was Adam Van Noort, his master,* and the master of Jordaens; around him are his contemporaries, educated in other studios, and whose invention is as spontaneous as his own—Jordaens, Crayer, Gerard Zeghers, Rombouts, Abraham Janssens, and Van Roose; after him come his pupils—Van Thulden, Diepenbecke, Van den Hoeck, Corneille Schut, Boyermans, Van Dyck, the greatest of all, and Van Oost of Bruges; alongside of him are the great animal, flower and still-life painters—Snyders, John Fyt, the Jesuit Seghers, and an entire school of famous engravers—Soutman, Vorsterman, Bolswert, Pontius and Vischer; the same sap fructifies all these branches, the lesser as well as the greater, while we must add, again, the perva-

---

* See the admirable "Miraculous Draft," by Van Noort, in St. James, at Antwerp.

ding sympathies and the national admiration. It is plain that an art like this is not the effect of one accidental cause but of a general development, and of this we have full assurance when, considering the work itself, we remark the concordances which assimilate it with its *milieu.*

On the one side it resumes or follows the traditions of Italy, and is seen at a glance to be pagan and Catholic. It is supported by churches and convents; it represents Biblical and evangelical scenes; the subject is edifying; and the engraver deliberately places at the bottom of his engravings pious maxims and moral problems. And yet, in fact, there is nothing Christian about it but its name; all mystic or ascetic sentiment is banished; its Madonnas, martyrs and confessors, its Christs and apostles are superb florid bodies restricted to the life of the flesh; its paradise is an Olympus of well-fed Flemish deities revelling in muscular activity; they are large, vigorous, plump and content, and make a jovial and magnificent display as in a national festival or at a princely entry. The Church, it is true, baptizes this last flower of the old mythology with becoming forms, but it is only baptism, and this is frequently wanting. Apollos, Jupiters, Castors, Pollux and Venus, all the ancient divinities, revive under their veritable names in the palaces of the kings and the great which they decorate. This is owing to religion, here as in Italy, consisting of rites. Rubens goes to mass every morning, and presents a picture in order to obtain indulgences; after which he falls back upon his own poetic feeling for natural life and, in the same style, paints a lusty Magdalen and a plump Siren; under the Catholic varnish the heart and the intellect, all social ways and observances are pagan. On the other side, this art is truly Flemish; everything issues from and centres on a mother idea which is new and national; it is harmonious, spontaneous and original; in this respect it contrasts with the foregoing which is only a discordant imitation. From Greece to Florence, from Florence to Venice, from Venice to Antwerp, every step of the passage can be traced. The conception of man and of life goes on decreasing in nobleness and increasing in breadth. Rubens is to Titian what Titian was to Raphael, and Raphael to

Phidias. Never did artistic sympathy clasp nature in such an open and universal embrace. Ancient boundaries, already often extended, seem removed purposely to expose an infinite career. There is no respect for historic proprieties; he groups together allegoric with real figures, and cardinals with a naked Mercury. There is no deference to the moral order; he fills the ideal heaven of mythology and of the gospel with coarse or mischievous characters; a Magdalen resembling a nurse, and a Ceres whispering some pleasant gossip in her neighbor's ear. There is no dread of exciting physical sensibility; he pushes the horrible to extremes, athwart all the tortures for the punishment of the flesh and all the contortions of howling agony. There is no fear of offending moral delicacy; his Minerva is a shrew who can fight, his Judith a butcher's wife familiar with blood, and his Paris a jocose expert and a dainty amateur. To translate into words the ideas vociferously proclaimed by his Suzannas, his Magdalens, his St. Sebastians, his Graces and his Sirens, in all his *kermesses*, divine and human, ideal or real, Christian or pagan, would require the terms of Rabelais. Through him all the animal instincts of human nature appear on the stage; those which had been excluded as gross he reproduces as true, and in him as in nature they encounter the others. Nothing is wanting but the pure and the noble; the whole of human nature is in his grasp, save the loftiest heights. Hence it is that his creativeness is the vastest we have seen, comprehending as it does all types, Italian cardinals, Roman emperors, contemporary citizens, peasants and cowherds, along with the innumerable diversities stamped on humanity by the play of natural forces and which more than fifteen hundred pictures did not suffice to exhaust.

For the same reason, in the representation of the body, he comprehended more profoundly than any one the essential characteristic of organic life; he surpasses in this the Venetians, as they surpass the Florentines; he feels still better than they that flesh is a changeable substance in a constant state of renewal; and such, more than any other, is the Flemish body, lymphatic, sanguine and voracious, more fluid, more rapidly tending to accretion and waste than those whose dry fibre and radical temperance preserve permanent tissues. Hence it is that nobody has depicted its contrasts in stronger relief, nor as visibly shown the decay and bloom of life—at one time the dull flabby corpse, a genuine clinical mass, empty of blood and substance, livid, blue and mottled through suffering, a clot of blood on the mouth, the eye glassy and the feet and hands clayish, swollen and deformed because death seized them first; at another the freshness of living carnations, the handsome, blooming and smiling athlete, the mellow suppleness of a yielding torso in the form of a well-fed adolescent, the soft rosy cheeks and placid candor of a girl whose blood was never quickened or eyes bedimmed by thought, flocks of dimpled cherubs and merry cupids, the delicacy, the folds, the exquisite melting rosiness of infantile skin, seemingly the petal of a flower moistened with dew and impregnated with morning light. In like manner in the representation of soul and action he appreciated more keenly than any one the essential feature of animal and moral life, that is to say the instantaneous movement which it is the aim of the plastic arts to

7*

seize on the wing. In this again he surpasses the Venetians as they surpassed the Florentines. Nobody
has endowed figures with such spirit, with a gesture
so impulsive, with an impetuosity so abandoned and
furious, such an universal commotion and tempest
of swollen and writhing muscles in one single effort.
His personages speak; their repose itself is suspen-
ded on the verge of action; we feel what they have
just accomplished and what they are about to do.
The present with them is impregnated with the past
and big with the future; not only the whole face but
the entire attitude conspires to manifest the flowing
stream of their thought, feeling and complete being;
we hear the inward utterance of their emotion; we
might repeat the words to which they give expression. The most fleeting and most subtle shades of
sentiment belong to Rubens; in this respect he is a
treasure for novelist and psychologist; he took note
of the passing refinements of moral expression as well
as of the soft volume of sanguine flesh; no one has
gone beyond him in knowledge of the living organism and of the animal man. Endowed with this sentiment and skill he was capable, in conformity with

the aspirations and needs of his restored nation, of amplifying the forces he found around and within himself, all that underlie, preserve and manifest the overflow and triumph of existence; on the one hand gigantic joints, herculean shapes and shoulders, red and colossal muscles, bearded and truculent heads, over-nourished bodies teeming with succulence, the luxurious display of white and rosy flesh; on the other, the rude instincts which impel human nature to seek food, drink, strife and pleasure, the savage fury of the combatant, the enormity of the big-bellied Silenus, the sensual joviality of the Faun, the abandonment of that lovely creature without conscience and "fat with sin," the boldness, the energy, the broad joyousness, the native goodness, the organic serenity of the national type. He heightens these effects again through their composition and the accessories with which he surrounds them—magnificence of lustrous silks, embroidered simarres and golden brocades, groups of naked figures, modern costumes and antique draperies, an inexhaustible accumulation of arms, standards, colonnades, Venetian stairways, temples, canopies, ships, animals, and

ever novel and imposing scenery, as if outside of
ordinary nature he possessed the key of a thousand
times richer nature, whereon his magician's hand
could forever draw without the freedom of his imagination ending in confusion, but on the contrary
with a jet so vigorous and a prodigality so national
that his most complicated productions seem like the
irresistible outflow of a surfeited brain. Like an
Indian deity at leisure he relieves his fecundity by
creating worlds, and from the matchless folds and
hues of his tossed simarres to the snowy whites of
his flesh, or the pale silkiness of his blonde tresses,
there is no tone in any of his canvasses which does
not appear there purposely to afford him delight.

There is only one Rubens in Flanders, as there
is only one Shakespeare in England. Great as the
others are, they are deficient in some one element of
his genius. Crayer has not his audacity nor his
excess ; he paints beauty calm,* sympathetic and
content along with requisite effects of bright and
mellow color. Jordaens has not his regal grandeur

---

* See at Ghent his "St. Rosalie," at Bruges his "Adoration of the
Shepherds," and at Rennes his "Lazarus."

and his heroic poetic feeling; he paints with vinous color stunted colossi, crowded groups and turbulent plebeians. Van Dyck has not, like him, the love of power and of life for life itself; more refined, more chivalric, born with a sensitive and even melancholy nature, elegiac in his sacred subjects, aristocratic in his portraits, he depicts with less glowing and more sympathetic color noble, tender and charming figures whose generous and delicate souls are filled with sweet and sad emotions unknown to his master.* His works are the first indication of the coming change. After 1660 he is already prominent. The generation whose energy and aspirations had inspired the grand picturesque revery, faded away man by man; Crayer and Jordaens alone, by merely living, kept art up for twenty years. The nation, reviving for a moment, falls backward; its renaissance never perfects itself. The archducal sovereigns, through whom it had become an independent state, ended in 1633; it reverts back to a Spanish province under a governor sent from Madrid. The treaty of 1648 closes the Scheldt to it, and completes

---

* See, especially, his sacred works at Malines and Antwerp.

the ruin of her commerce. Louis XIV. dismembers her, and on three occasions deprives her of portions of her territory. Four successive wars trample over her for thirty years; friends and enemies, Spaniards, French, English and Hollanders live upon her; the treaties of 1715 convert the Dutch into her purveyors and tax-gatherers. At this moment, become Austrian, she refuses the subsidy; but the elders of the states are imprisoned, and the chief one, Anneessens, dies on the scaffold; this is the last and a feeble echo of the mighty voice of Van Artevelde. Henceforth the country subsides into a simple province in which people keep soul and body together and only care to live. At the same time, and through a reaction, the national imagination declines. The school of Rubens degenerates; with Beyermans, Van Herp, John Erasmus Quellin, the second Van Oost, Deyster and John Van Orley we see originality and energy disappearing; coloring grows weak or becomes affected; attenuated types incline to prettiness; expression is either sentimental or mawkish; the personages occupying the great canvas, instead of filling it are dispersed, the intervals being supplied with architecture; the vein is exhausted; painting is mere routine or a mannered imitation of the Italian school. Many betake themselves to foreign countries. Philippe de Champagne is director of the Academy of the Fine Arts at Paris and becomes French in mind and country; still more, a spiritualist and Jansenist, a conscientious and skilful painter of grave and thoughtful spirit. Gerard de Lairesse becomes a disciple of the Italians—a classic, academic and erudite painter of costume and historic and mythologic resemblances. The logical reason assumes empire in the arts, having already obtained it in social matters. Two pictures in the Musée of Ghent equally display the change in painting and the change in society. Both represent princely entrées, one in 1666 and the other in 1717. The first, of a beautiful ruddy tone, shows the last of the men of the grand epoch, their cavalier air, their powerful frame, their capacity for physical endeavor, their rich decorative costumes, their horses with with flowing manes—here nobles related to Van Dyck's seigniors, and there pikemen in buff and cuirass kindred to the soldiers of Wallestein—in short, the last remains of the heroic and picturesque age. The second, cold and pale in tone, shows highly refined, softened, Frenchified beings—gentlemen clever at salutation, women of fashion conscious of their appearance, in brief, the imported drawing-room system and foreign modes of demeanor. During the fifty years separating the former from the latter both the national art and the national spirit vanished.

IV.

Whilst the Southern provinces, henceforth subject and Catholic, followed the Italian road in art, and represented on their canvasses the mythological epos of the grand and heroic nude figure, the provinces of the North, becoming free and Protestant, developed their life and art in another direction. The climate is more rainy and colder, and for this reason the presence of the nude is a rarer and less sympathetic thing. The Germanic race is chaster, and through this quality the mind is less inclined to appreciate classic art, as it was conceived of by the Italian renaissance. Life is more difficult, more laborious, and more economic; man, therefore, accustomed to effort, to forethought and to a methodical self-government, has more trouble in comprehending the fascinating dream of a sensuous and full-blown existence. We can imagine the Dutch citizen in his home after the day's toil at his business. His dwelling consists of small apartments, somewhat resembling the state-rooms of a ship; it would be a troublesome matter to suspend on the walls the large pictures decorating the saloons of an Italian palace; its owner's chief requirements are cleanliness and comfort; with these he is content and does not insist on decoration. According to the Venetian ambassadors, " they are so moderate that, even with the richest, one sees no unusual pomp or luxury. . . . . They make no use of retainers or silken habits, very little silver-ware, and no tapestry in their houses; the household numbers a very few and is very limited. Outside and inside, in dress and in other matters, all maintain the true moderation of small fortunes, nothing superfluous being perceptible." * When the Earl of Leicester came to take command in Holland in the name of Elizabeth, and Spinola arrived to negotiate peace for the King of Spain, their regal magnificence formed a striking contrast and even provoked scandal. The head of the republic, William the Taciturn, the hero of the age, wore an old mantle which a student would have pro-

---

* Motley's "United Netherlands," Vol. IV. p. 551. Report of Contarini, 1609.

nounced threadbare, with a pourpoint like it, unbut-
toned, and a woollen waistcoat resembling that of a
bargeman. In the next century the adversary of
Louis XIV., the grand pensioner John de Witt kept
only one domestic; everybody could approach him;
he imitated his illustrious predecessor, who lived
cheek-by-jowl with "brewers and bourgeois." We
find yet at the present day, in their social ways,
many an indication of ancient sobriety. It is clear
that with such characters there is but little room for
the decorative and voluptuous instincts which elsewhere in Europe fashioned aristocratic show, and
rendered comprehensible the pagan poesy of beautiful bodies.

The opposite instincts, in effect, predominate.
Relieved of the drawback of the Southern provinces,
Holland, at the end of the sixteenth century, suddenly and with extraordinary energy turns in the
direction of its natural proclivities. Primitive incli-
nations and faculties appear with the most striking results; they are not a new birth, but simply
a revelation. Good observers had detected them
a hundred and fifty years before. "Friesland is

free," said Pope Æneas Sylvius,* " lives in her own
fashion, will not endure foreign empire, and has no
desire to dominate over others. The Frieslander
does not hesitate to face death in behalf of liberty.
This spirited people, used to arms, of large and
robust frames, calm and intrepid in disposition,
glories in her freedom notwithstanding that Philip,
Duke of Burgundy, proclaims himself lord of the
country. They detest military and feudal arro-
gance, and tolerate no man who seeks to raise his
head above his fellows. Their magistrates are
elected annually by themselves, and are obliged to
administer public matters with equity. . . . They
severely punish licentiousness among women . . .
They scarcely admit an unmarried priest lest he
should corrupt the wife of another, regarding con-
tinence as a difficult thing and beyond the natural
powers." Every Germanic conception of state, marriage and religion are here visible in germ, and
forecast the final flowering of the republic and of
Protestantism. Subjected to trial by Philip II.
they offer to sacrifice beforehand "their lives and

---

* Cosmographia, p. 421

their property." A small population of traders,
lost on a mud-heap at the extremity of an empire
more vast and more feared than that of Napoleon,
resisted, subsisted and increased under the weight
of the colossus who tried to crush her. Their sieges
are all admirable; citizens and women, supported
by a few hundreds of soldiers, arrest an entire army
before ruined ramparts, the best troops in Europe,
the greatest generals and the most skilful engin-
eers; and this remnant of emaciated people, after
feeding on rats, boiled leaves and leather for
months, determine, rather than surrender, to place
the infirm in the centre of a square and go forth to
die in the intrenchments of the enemy. The details
of this war must be read in order to realize the
extent to which man's patience, coolness and energy
may be carried.* On the sea a Dutch vessel is
blown up rather than strike its flag, while their voy-
ages of discovery, colonization and conquest, in
Nova Zembla, India and Brazil, by the way of the
Straits of Magellan, are as magnificent as their

---

* Among others the capture of Bois-le-Duc by Héraugière and sixty
nine volunteers.

combats. The more we demand of human nature
the more she gives; her faculties are exalted in
their exercise, while the limits to her power of
doing and suffering are no longer perceptible.
Finally, in 1609, after thirty years warfare, the cause
is won. Spain recognizes their independence, and
during the whole of the seventeenth century they
are to play a most prominent part in the affairs of
Europe. No power can make them yield, neither
Spain during a second war of twenty-seven years,
nor Cromwell, nor Charles II., nor England combined with France, nor the fresh and formidable
power of Louis XIV.; after three wars their ambassadors are all to be seen in humble and fruit-
less entreaty at Gertruydenberg, and the grand-
pensioner Heinsius, is to become one of the three
potentates to control the destinies of Europe.

Internally their government is as good as their
external position is exalted. For the first time in
the world conscience is free and the rights of the citizens are respected. Their state consists of a community of provinces voluntarily united, which, each
within its own borders, maintains with a degree of

perfection unknown till then the security of the public and the liberty of the individual. "They all love liberty," says Parival in 1660; "no one among them is allowed to beat or abuse another, while the women servants have so many privileges their masters, even, dare not strike them." Full of his admiration, he repeatedly insists on this wonderful respect for human personality. "There is not to-day a province in the world which enjoys so much liberty as Holland, with so just a harmony that the little cannot be imposed upon by the great, nor the poor by the rich and opulent . . . The moment a seignior brings into this country any serfs or slaves they are free; yes, and the money he laid out in their purchase is lost . . . The inhabitants of a village having paid what they owe are as free as the inhabitants of a city . . . And above all each is king in his own house, it being a very serious crime to have done violence to a bourgeois in his own domicile." Everybody can leave the country when he pleases, and take all the money he pleases with him. The roads are safe day and night even for a man traveling alone. The master is not allowed to retain a domestic against his will. Nobody is troubled on account of his religion. One is free to say what he chooses, "even of the magistrates," and to denounce them. Equality is fundamental. "Those who hold office obtain consideration rather through fair dealing than advance themselves over others by a proud bearing." A nation like this cannot fail to be prosperous; when man is both just and energetic the rest comes to him as surplus. At the beginning of the War of Independence the population of Amsterdam was 70,000; in 1618 it was 300,000. The Venetian ambassadors reported that people swarmed in the streets every hour of the day as at a fair. The city increased two-thirds; a surface equal to the size of a man's foot was worth a gold ducat. The country is as good as the city. Nowhere is the peasant so rich and so able to derive advantage from the soil; one village possesses four thousand cows; an ox weighs two thousand pounds. A farmer offers his daughter to Prince Maurice with a dowry of one hundred thousand florins. Nowhere are industrial pursuits and manufactures so perfect; cloths, mirrors, sugar-refineries, porcelain, pottery, rich stuffs of silk, satin and

brocade, iron-ware and ship-rigging. They supply
Europe with half of its luxuries and nearly all its
transportation. A thousand vessels traverse the
Baltic in quest of raw material. Eight hundred
boats are engaged in the herring fishery. Vast companies monopolize trade with India, China and
Japan; Batavia is the centre of a Dutch empire; at
this moment, 1609, Holland on the sea and in the
world is what England was in the time of Napoleon.
She has a marine of one hundred thousand sailors; in
war time she can man two thousand vessels; fifty
years after she maintains herself against the combined fleets of France and England; year after year
the great stream of her success and prosperity is
seen to increase. But its source is yet more bountiful than the stream itself; that which sustains her is
an excess of courage, reason, abnegation, will and
genius; "this people," say the Venetian ambassadors, "are inclined to labor and industry to such a
degree that no enterprise is too difficult for them to
succeed in . . . They are born for work and for privation, and all are doing something, some one way and
some another." Much production and light con-

8

sumption is the mode of growth of public prosperity. The poorest, "in their small and humble habitations," have all necessary things. The richest in their fine houses avoid the superfluous and ostentation; nobody is in want, and nobody abuses; every one is employed with his hands or his mind. "All things are made profitable," says Parival; "there are none, even to those who gather ordure out of the canals who do not earn half-a-crown a day. Children even who are learning their trades almost earn their bread at the start. They are so inimical to bad government and to indolence that they have places in which the magistrates imprison idlers and vagabonds, also those who do not properly attend to their business—the complaints of wives or family relations being a sufficient warrant, and in these places they are obliged to work and earn their subsistence whether they will or not." The convents are transformed into hospitals, asylums and homes for orphans, the former revenues of lazy monks supporting invalids, the aged, and widows and children of soldiers and sailors lost in war. The army is so efficient that any of its soldiers might serve as captain in an Italian army, while no Italian captain would be admitted in it as a common soldier. In culture and instruction, as well as in the arts of organization and of government, the Dutch are two centuries ahead of the rest of Europe. Scarcely a man, woman or child can be found who does not know how to read and write (1609). Every village has a public school. In a bourgeois family all the boys read Latin and all the girls French. Many people write and converse in several foreign languages. It is not owing to simple precaution, to habits of laying up and calculations of utility, but they appreciate the dignity of science. Leyden, to which the States-General propose a recompense, after its heroic defense, demands a University; no pains are spared to attract to it the greatest savans of Europe. The States themselves unite, and through Henry IV. cause letters to be sent to Scaliger, who is poor and a professor, begging him to honor the city with his presence; no lessons will be required of him; they merely wish him to come and converse with the erudites, direct their efforts, and allow the nation to participate in the fame of his writings. Under this regime Leyden becomes the most renowned school in Europe; she has two thousand students; philosophy hunted out of France finds refuge there; during the seventeenth century Holland is the first of thoughtful countries. The positive sciences here find their native soil, or the land of their adoption. Scaliger, Justus Lepsius, Saumaisius, Meursius, the two Heinsius, the two Dousa, Marnix de Ste-Aldegonde, Hugo Grotius and Snellius preside over learning, laws, physics and mathematics. The Elzevirs carry on printing. Lindshoten and Mercator furnish instruction to travellers and develop geographical science. Hooft, Bor and Meteren write the history of the nation. Jacob Cats provides its poetry. Theology, which is the philosophy of the day, takes up, with Arminius and Gomar, the question of grace, and, even in the smallest villages, agitates the minds of peasants and bourgeois. The Synod of Dordrecht at length in 1609 constitutes the œcumenical council of the Reformation. To this primacy of speculative intellect add that of practical genius: from Barnevelt to De Witt, from William the Taciturn to William III., from Heemskerck the admiral to Von Tromp and De Ruyter, a sequence of superior men are at the head of art and business matters. It is under these circumstances that the national art appears. All the great original painters are born in the first thirty years of the seventeenth century, after grave danger had passed away, when the final victory was assured, when man, sensible of great things accomplished, points out to his children the onward path which has been cleared by his vigorous arm and stout heart. Here, as elsewhere, the artist is the offspring of the hero. The faculties employed in the creation of a real world, now that the work is accomplished, reach beyond and are employed in the creation of an imaginary world. Man has done too much to go back to school; the field spread out before him and around him has been peopled by his activity; it is so glorious and so fecund he can long dwell upon and admire it; he need no longer subdue his own thought to a foreign thought; he seeks and discovers his own peculiar sentiment; he dares to confide himself to it, to pursue it to the end, to imitate nobody, to derive all from himself, to invent with no

other guide but the voiceless preferences of his own
senses and his own affections. His inner forces, his
fundamental aptitudes, his primitive and hereditary
instincts drawn out and fortified by experience continue to operate after his experience, and, when they
have formed a nation they form an art.

Let us consider this art. It manifests through colors and forms all the instincts that have just appeared in actions and in works. So long as the
seven provinces of the North and the ten provinces
of the South formed but one nation they had but one
school of art. Engelbrecht, Lucas of Leyden, John
Schoreel, the elder Heemskerck, Corneille of Harlem,
Bloemaert and Goltzius paint in the same style as
their contemporaries of Bruges and Antwerp. There
is not as yet a distinct Dutch school, because there is
not as yet a distinct Belgian school. At the time
when the War of Independence begins the painters
of the North are laboring to convert themselves
into Italians like the painters of the South. After
the year 1600, however, there is a complete change
in painting as in other things. The rising sap of the
nation gives predominance to the national instincts.

Nudities are no longer visible; the ideal figure, the beautiful human animal living in full sunshine, the noble symmetry of limbs and attitude, the grand allegoric or mythological picture is no longer adapted to Germanic taste. Calvanism, moreover, which now rules, excludes it from its temples, and amidst this population of earnest and economic laborers there is no seigneurial display, no widespread and grandiose epicureanism which, elsewhere, in the palaces and in proximity to luxurious silver, liveries and furniture, demands the sensual and pagan canvas. When Amelia of Solm desires to raise a monument in this style to her husband, the stadtholder Frederic Henry, she is obliged to send to Orangesaal for the Flemish artists Van Thulden and Jordaens. To these realistic imaginations and amidst these republican customs, in this land where a shoemaking privateer can become vice-admiral, the most interesting figure is one of its own citizens, a man of flesh and blood, not draped or undraped like a Greek, but in his own costume and ordinary attitude, some good magistrate or valiant officer. The heroic style is suited to but one thing, the great portraits which decorate the town-halls and public institutions in commemoration of services rendered. We see, in fact, a new kind of picture make its appearance here, the vast canvas on which are displayed five, ten, twenty and thirty full-length portraits as large as life, hospital directors, arquebusiers on target excursions, syndics assembled around a table, officers offering toasts at a banquet, professors giving clinical lectures, all grouped according to their pursuits, and all presented to view with the costume, arms, banners, accessories and surroundings belonging to their actual life; it is a veritable historical picture, the most instructive and most impressive of all, where Franz Hals, Rembrandt, Govaêrt Flinck, Ferdinand Bol, Theodore de Keyser and John Ravenstein depict the heroic age of their nation, where sensible, energetic and loyal heads possess the nobleness of power and of conscience, where the fine costume of the renaissance, the scarfs, the buff vests, the frills, the lace collars, the pourpoints and the black mantles throw their gravity and brilliancy around the solid portliness of the stout forms and frank expressions of the faces, where the artist, now through the virile simplicity of his means, now through the strength of his convictions, becomes the equal of his heroes.

Such is painting for the public; there now remains painting for private life, that which decorates the houses of individuals, and which, in its dimensions as well as subjects, conforms to the condition and character of its purchasers. "There is no bourgeois so poor," says Parival, "who does not liberally indulge his taste this way." A baker pays six hundred florins for a single figure by Van der Meer of Delft. This, along with a neat and agreeable interior, constitutes their luxury; "they do not grudge money in this direction, which they rather save on their stomachs." The national instinct re-appears here the same as revealed in the first epoch with John Van Eyck, Quintin Matsys, and Lucas of Leyden; and it is emphatically the national instinct, for it is so deep and so active that, even in Belgium, in close proximity to mythological and decorative art, it runs through the Breughels and Teniers like a small brook alongside of a broad river. It exacts and provokes the representation of man as he is and life as it is, both as the eye encounters them, citizens,

8*

peasants, cattle, shops, taverns, rooms, streets and landscapes. There is no need to transform them in order to ennoble them; they are satisfied if they are worthy of interest. Nature, in herself, whatever she may be, whether human, animal, vegetable or inanimate, with all her irregularities, minutiæ and omissions, is inherently right, and, when comprehended, people love and delight to contemplate her. The object of art is not to change her, but to interpret her; through sympathy it renders her beautiful. Thus understood, painting may represent the housekeeper spinning in her rural cot, the carpenter planing on his work-bench, the surgeon dressing a rustic's arm, the cook spitting a chicken, the rich dame washing herself; all sorts of interiors, from the hovel to the drawing-room; all sorts of types, from the rubicund visage of the deep drinker to the placid smile of the well-bred damsel; every scene of refined or rustic life—a card-party in a gilded saloon, a peasant's carouse in a bare tavern, skaters on a frozen canal, cows drinking from a trough, vessels at sea, the entire and infinite diversities of sky, earth, water, darkness and daylight. Terburg, Metzu, Gerard

Dow, Van der Meer of Delft, Adrian Brouwer,
Schalcken, Franz Mieris, Jan Steen, Wouverman,
the two Ostades, Wynants, Cuyp, Van der Neer,
Ruysdael, Hobbema, Paul Potter, Backhuysen, the
two Vanderveldes, Philip of Kœnig, Van der Heyden,
and how many more! There is no school in which
artists of original talent are so numerous. When
the domain of art consists, not of a small summit,
but of the wide expanse of life, it offers to each mind
a distinct field; the ideal is narrow, and inhabited
only by two or three geniuses; the real is immense,
and provides places for fifty men of talent. A tranquil and pleasing harmony emanates from all these
performances. We are conscious of repose in looking at them. The spirit of the artist, like that of his
figures, is in equilibrium; we should be quite content
and comfortable in his picture. We realize that his
imagination does not go beyond. It seems as if he,
like his personages, were satisfied with mere living.
Nature appears to him excellent; all he cares for is
to add some arrangement, some tone side by side
with another, some effect of light, some choice of
attitude. In her presence he is like a happy-wedded

Hollander in the presence of his spouse; he would not wish her otherwise; he loves her through affectionate routine and innate concordance; at the utmost his chief requirement of her will be to wear at some festival her red frock instead of the blue one. He bears no resemblance to our painters, expert observers taught by æsthetic and philosophic books and journals, who depict the peasant and the laborer the same as the Turk and the Arab, that is to say, as curious animals and interesting specimens; who charge their landscapes with the subtleties, refinements and emotions of poets and civilians in order to rid themselves of the mute and dreamy revery of life. He is of a more näive order; he is not dislocated or over-excited by excessive cerebral activity; as compared to us he is an artizan; when he takes up painting he has none other than picturesque intentions; he is less affected by unforeseen and striking detail than by simple and leading general traits. His work, on this account, healthier and less poignant, appeals to less cultivated natures, and pleases the greater number. Among all these painters, two only—Ruysdael, in spiritual finesse and marked superiority of education, and Rembrandt especially, in a peculiar structure of the eye and a wonderfully wild genius—developed, beyond their age and nation, up to the common instincts which bind the Germanic nations together and pave the way for modern sentiments. The latter, constantly collecting his materials, living in solitude and borne along by the growth of an extraordinary faculty, lived, like our Balzac, a magician and a visionary in a world fashioned by his own hand and of which he alone possessed the key. Superior to all painters in the native delicacy and keenness of his optical perceptions, he comprehended this truth and adhered to it in all its consequences that, to the eye, the essence of a visible object consists of the spot (*tache*), that the simplest color is infinitely complex, that every visual sensation is the product of its elements coupled with its surroundings, that each object on the field of sight is but a single spot modified by others, and that, in this wise, the principal feature of a picture is the ever-present, tremulous, colored atmosphere into which figures are plunged like fishes in the sea. He rendered this atmosphere palpable, and revealed to us its mysterious and thronging population; he impregnated it with the light of his own country—a feeble, yellow illumination like that of a lamp in a cellar; he felt the mournful struggle between it and shadow, the weakness of vanishing rays dying away in gloom, the tremulousness of reflections vainly clinging to gleaming walls, the sum of that vague multitude of half-darks which, invisible to ordinary gaze, seem in his paintings and etchings to form a submarine world dimly visible through an abyss of waters. On emerging from this obscurity the full light, to his eyes, proved a dazzling shower; he felt as if it were flashes of lightning, or some magical effulgence, or as myriads of beaming darts. He found accordingly, in the inanimate world the completest and most expressive drama, all contrasts and all conflicts, whatever is overwhelming and painfully lugubrious in night, whatever is most fleeting and saddest in ambiguous shadow, whatever is most violent and most irresistible in the irruption of daylight. This done, all that remained was to impose the human drama on the natural drama; a stage thus fashioned indicates of itself its own characters.

The Greeks and Italians had known of man and
of life only the straightest and tallest stems, the
healthy flower blooming in sunshine; he saw the
root, everything which crawls and moulders in
shadow, the stunted and deformed sprouts, the
obscure crowd of the poor, the Jewry of Amsterdam, the slimy, suffering populace of a large city
and unfavorable climate, the bandy-legged beggar,
the bloated idiot, the bald skull of an exhausted
craftsman, the pallid features of the sick, the whole
of that grovelling array of evil passions and hideous
miseries which infest our various civilizations like
worms in a rotten plank. Once on this road he
could comprehend the religion of grief, the genuine
Christianity; he could interpret the Bible as if he
were a Lollard; he could recognize the eternal Christ
as present now as formerly, as living in a cellar or
tavern of Holland as beneath a Jerusalem sun; the
healer and consoler of the miserable, alone capable
of saving them because as poor and as miserable as
themselves. He too, through a reaction, was conscious of pity; by the side of others who seem
painters of the aristocracy he is of the people; he

is, at least, the most humane; his broader sympathies embrace more of nature fundamentally; no ugliness repels him, no craving for joyousness or nobleness hides from him the lowest depths of truth. Hence it is that, free of all trammels and guided by the keen sensibility of his organs, he has succeeded in portraying in man not merely the general structure and the abstract type which answers for classic art, but again that which is peculiar and profound in the individual, the infinite and indefinable complications of the moral being, the whole of that changeable imprint which concentrates instantaneously on a face the entire history of a soul and which Shakespeare alone saw with an equally prodigious lucidity. In this respect he is the most original of modern artists, and forges one end of the chain of which the Greeks forged the other; the rest of the masters, Florentine, Venetian and Flemish, stand between them; and when, nowadays, our over-excited sensibility, our extravagant curiosity in the pursuit of subtleties, our unsparing search of the true, our divination of the remote and the obscure in human nature, seeks for predecessors and masters, it is in him and in Shakespeare that Balzac and Delacroix are able to find them.

A blooming period like this is transient for the reason that the sap which produces it is exhausted by its production. Towards 1667, after the naval defeats of England, slight indications show the growing change in the manners, customs and sentiments which had stimulated the national art. The prosperity is too great. Already, in 1660, Parival, speaking of this, grows ecstatic in every chapter; the companies of the East and West Indies declare dividends to their stockholders of forty and fifty per cent. Heroes become citizens; Parival notices the thirst for gain among those of the highest class. And more, " they detest duels, contentions and quarrels, and commonly assert that well-off people never fight." They want to enjoy themselves, and the houses of the great, which the Venetian ambassadors early in the century find so bare and so simple, become luxurious; among the leading citizens there are found tapestries, high-priced pictures and " gold and silver-plate." The rich interiors of Terburg and Metzu show us the new-found elegance—the light silk dresses, velvet bodices, the gems, the pearls, the hangings honey-combed with gold, and the lofty chimneys with marble columns. Ancient energy relaxes. When Louis XIV. invades the country in 1672 he finds no resistance. The army has been neglected; their troops are disbanded; their towns surrender at the first blow; four French cavaliers take Muyden which is the key to the floodgates; the States-General implore peace on any terms. The national sentiment degenerates, at the same time, in the arts. Taste becomes transformed. Rembrandt in 1669 dies poor, almost without anybody's knowledge; the new-found luxury is satisfied with foreign models obtained from France and Italy. Already, during the most flourishing epoch, a number of painters had gone to Rome to paint small figures and landscapes; Jan Both, Berghem, Karl Dujardin, and many others—Wouvermans himself—form a half-Italian school alongside of the national school. But this school was spontaneous and natural; amid the mountains, ruins, structures and rags of the South the vapory whiteness of the atmosphere, the geniality of the figures, the mellow carnations, the gayety

and good humor of the painter denote the persistency and freedom of the Dutch instinct. On the
other hand, we see at this moment this instinct becoming enfeebled under the invasion of fashion. On
the Kaisergracht and the Heeregracht rise grand
hotels in the style of Louis XIV., while the Flemish
painter who founded the academic school, Gerard de
Lairesse, comes to decorate them with his learned
allegories and hybrid mythologies. The national
art, it is true, does not at once surrender; it is prolonged by a succession of masterpieces up to the
first years of the eighteenth century; at the same
time the national sentiment, aroused by humiliation
and danger, excites a popular revolution, heroic
sacrifices, the inundation of the country, and all the
successes which afterwards ensue. But these very
successes complete the ruin of the energy and enthusiasm which this temporary revival had stimulated.
During the whole of the war of the Spanish succession, Holland, whose stadtholder became King of
England, is sacrificed to its ally; after the treaty of
1713 she loses her maritime supremacy, falls to the
second rank of powers, and, finally, still lower;

Frederic the Great is soon able to say that she is dragged in the wake of England like a sloop behind a man-of-war. France tramples on her during the war of the Austrian succession; later, England imposes on her the right of search and deprives her of the coast of Coromandel. Finally, Prussia steps in, overwhelms the republican party and establishes the stadtholdership. Like all the weak she is hustled by the strong, and, after 1789, conquered and reconquered. What is worse she gives up and is content to remain a good commercial banking-house. Already in 1723 her historian, John Leclerc, a refugee, openly ridicules the valiant seamen who, during the War of Independence, blew themselves up rather than strike their flag.* In 1732, another historian declares that " the Dutch think of nothing but the accumulation of riches." After 1748 both the army and the fleet are allowed to decline. In 1787 the Duke of Brunswick brings the country under subjection almost without striking a blow. What a distance between sentiments of this cast and those of

---

* " This good captain belonged to those who die for fear of dying. If God forgives such people it is because they are out of their mind."

the companions of William the Taciturn, De Ruyter
and Von Tromp! Hence it is that, through an admirable concordance, we see picturesque invention
terminating with practical energy. In ten years
after the commencement of the eighteenth century
all the great painters are dead. Already for a generation a decline is manifest in the impoverished
style, in the more limited imagination and in more
minute finish of Franz Mieris, Schalcken, and the rest.
One of these, Adrian Van der Werf, in his cold and
polished painting, his mythologies and nudities, his
ivory carnations, his impotent return to the Italian
style, bears witness to the Dutch oblivion of native
tastes and its own peculiar genius. His successors
resemble men who attempt to speak with nothing
to say; brought up by masters or famous parents,
Peter Van der Werf, Henry Van Limborch, Philip
Van Dyck, Mieris the younger, and another the
grandson, Nicholas Verkolie, and Constantine Nets-
cher repeat sentences they have heard, but like au-
tomatons. Talent survives only among painters of
accessories and flowers—Jacques de Witt, Rachel
Ruysch and Van Huysum—in a small way, which

requires less invention and which still lasts a few years, similar to a tenacious clump of bushes on a dry soil whereon all the great trees have died. This dies in its turn, and the ground remains vacant. It is the last evidence of the dependence which attaches individual originality to social life, and proportions the inventive faculties of the artist to the active energies of the nation.

THE END.